Read the Reviews!

Oh, the joy and the journey of watching a young child grow up! Within these pages lies a bridge between the children of God who are just starting life and those who are on the latter end. Debbie Bailey has recorded the inside story of how her grandchild has opened the windows of God's wisdom to her. Chock full of conundrums and humor, these 31 devotions offer an invitation to enter into God's ways and heart for us. Be prepared to reflect on your own life as Debbie reflects on hers and grandchild Reagan's.

- Reverend Cathy Eskew, PCUSA

Art Linkletter famously entertained us with "Kids say the darndest things." *In Divine Directions from the Booster Seat*, Debbie has handpicked her precious granddaughter's words and actions and triumphantly partnered them with teachings of our Lord. Each meditation guides the reader with thought provoking questions perfect for a Bible study group or individual reflection. Readers' heartstrings will be pulled with each story. I couldn't wait to turn to the next reading to pause, reflect, and relate to the featured scripture. This is a book you will want to keep close at hand and study more than once.

- Linda Manchee Kosich, early childhood educator

In *Divine Directions from the Booster Seat*, Debbie insightfully reminds us what it is like to be a child again as she transforms Reagan's simple observations into deeper truths in God's Word. This delightful book of meditations will bless you!

- Tricia Langley, retired chaplain

Divine Directions from the Booster Seat

Thirty-One Meditations from God through Reagan to Me and Now to You – Part Two

DEBORAH DENISON BAILEY

WESTBOW
PRESS®
A DIVISION OF THOMAS NELSON
& ZONDERVAN

WestBow Press books may be ordered through booksellers or by contacting:

WestBow Press
A Division of Thomas Nelson & Zondervan
1663 Liberty Drive
Bloomington, IN 47403
www.westbowpress.com
844-714-3454

Scripture quotations taken from The Holy Bible, New International Version® NIV® Copyright © 1973 1978 1984 2011 by Biblica, Inc. TM. Used by permission. All rights reserved worldwide.

ISBN: 978-1-6642-3994-4 (sc)
ISBN: 978-1-6642-3996-8 (hc)
ISBN: 978-1-6642-3995-1 (e)

Library of Congress Control Number: 2021913878

Print information available on the last page.

WestBow Press rev. date: 08/20/2021

Dedicated to

Without my amazing granddaughter, Reagan Marie Bailey, this series would not be possible! She inspires me to keep my eyes wide open to life's wonders which magnify the joys of loving her. Praise be to God!

Contents

Preface

This second book is a continuation of my recording the often times insightful and frequently amusing things that my precious granddaughter, Reagan, has said over the last couple of years. When I wrote the first book, *Divine Directions from the Car Seat*, there seemed to be more expressions that caught my ear. Now that she is getting older, her innocent musings are less frequent and I have been challenged to draw lessons from them. It is my hope and prayer that there will be even more opportunity for increased depth of contemplation in Part Two. Some thoughts have taken some very interesting turns!

It remains my high honor to give God the glory for all the messages He has directed me to record from Reagan's sweet morsels. She continues to inspire my husband (Bampa) and me to think beyond our own pre-conceived limits.

As well as preserving a legacy for Reagan, I trust I am being obedient to the Lord by continuing to make these meditations available to the public. By following the Lord's direction, I believe that all our paths become wider, thereby expanding the opportunity for others to choose to follow His lead. I pray that you will enjoy the ride!

A note before you start the journey...

Except for the first story in which Reagan is seven years old, the dates of these meditations are all listed in chronological order. I placed it first because it provides an insight to guide us through the rest of the book. Moreover, it also highlights the blessing of having a place of refuge to meditate and to acknowledge and give glory to our Creator God who uniquely fashions those provisions for each one of us. In the second story, *Dry Eyes*, you will meet five-year-old Reagan.

1 | Where is Your "Beach"?

June 21, 2021

I love the beach! As I walk the sandy shores and enjoy the ebb and flow of the ocean, I feel a deeply spiritual connection with our Creator God. I live in Colorado Springs, Colorado, so when I am able to visit the seashore, it is always a very special occasion for me.

One day while my seven-year-old granddaughter, Reagan, was playing in my backyard, she decided that she was going to surprise me with something she planned to create. She then proceeded to tell me that I could not watch her, and she would come get me when she was done. Having completed her project, she came and got me and instructed me to close my eyes as she carefully guided my steps along a path she had designed outside.

When we arrived at our destination, Reagan proudly stated, "Nana, this is your beach. I worked very hard on it for you."

My sweet little one knew how much I loved going to the beach. Even though we had not talked about it that day, she remembered. Her heart reached out to mine in such a loving way. I was overwhelmed!

On the side of my yard, I have a large pile of cut wood that sits on a bed of stones. Reagan had retrieved a large limb and propped it up vertically against the stack of wood. On top of the large limb were assembled several smaller sticks. Reagan informed me that was my umbrella for the beach. The stones represented the beach. On the side of the umbrella, she had laid two sticks on the ground, crossed them and put two medium-sized stones in front of the sticks. The stones were supposed to be the eyes for the seagull and the sticks were its body and wings. Under the umbrella was a large stone that was supposed to be a pillow for my head, followed by some cement bricks that were intended to be the place to lie down. Reagan very meticulously and thoughtfully included all these details of the beach for me.

Some time has passed now, and weather has taken its toll on the umbrella and the path to the beach, but I can't seem to tolerate the idea of tidying up the area. After all, it is my beach. It was crafted by my granddaughter whom I adore. I feel her heart there every single time I walk by the woodpile.

Similarly, I feel the presence of the Lord in a strong and mighty way when I am at the beach. Yes, there are other times when I know He is near. I don't have to travel to find Him, but when I do venture to the seashore, He greets me in a singular way.

I think many of us have places of refuge that are uniquely designed just for us. Not only does the Lord prepare places for us but, He also brings people into our lives who bless us and remind us of His greatness. The Lord used Reagan that day to bless me. I have a beach in my backyard now and I know He is there.

Where is *your* "beach"?

Key Thought

Where is your "beach"?

Scripture

"The LORD is my shepherd, I shall not want. He makes me lie down in green pastures, he leads me beside quiet waters, he restores my soul" (Psalm 23:1-3a).

Prayer

Thank You, dear Lord, for all creation! Thank You for the special places that You design for us. Thank You for knowing us and loving us. Thank You for people who touch our hearts and remind us of the countless ways You bless us. We know we don't have to travel to the seashore or to the top of a mountain to commune with You. Please help us to acknowledge the fact that You are always with us. We want to give You the glory and the honor You deserve. In the powerful name of Jesus we pray. Amen.

For Further Reflection

1. Do you have a special place of refuge that you feel the Lord designed just for you? Describe it.

2. Name the people whom God has placed in your life who have blessed you in countless ways.
3. Name the people in your life whom God has called you to serve.
4. Challenge: How can you add an extra measure of blessing to someone's life the way Reagan did by creating the beach for me?

Reagan's Gift of the Beach to Me
Photo by Deborah Denison Bailey, 2021

2 | Dry Eyes

October 8, 2018

When Reagan had her fourth birthday party, it did not turn out so well. More specifically, the pictures did not end up the way we all had hoped. When the time came to sing "Happy Birthday" and to blow out the candles, Reagan was trying not to cry, but her efforts failed. Earlier, she had been bumped a little bit too hard in the bounce house where the kids were all playing. She just could not get over her "ouchies", and she was extremely sad about it. Needless to say, it was all I could do not to cry with her. My heart was hurting with hers. Despite the total lack of Kodak moments, I took pictures anyway. I am rather sorry I did. To this day, every time I look at the photos, my heart is distressed that Reagan's special day was such a disappointment for her. Predictably, after a bit of time had passed and we had sung and eaten cake, she was back in the bounce house having the time of her life. However, being the sensitive and vulnerable nana that I am, I was not quite as resilient.

So when it came time for birthday number five to roll around, we were all preparing for it to be perfect. There was another bounce house in the backyard and surely there would be no mishaps or tears this time. No such luck. Ugh! A "big kid" managed to bump Reagan while they were all jumping and again there were more "ouchies", and the pathetic wailing began.

I thought to myself that I just could not handle another batch of photos featuring Reagan's miserable, sad face! I decided to talk to her. I stood outside the bounce house, and she sat alone inside it. With her head down and with big tears trickling down her face, she mournfully described her cheerless fate.

I sympathetically tried to examine her "ouchies" as I peered through the mesh of the bounce house. There were no noticeable red places anywhere. The wound was obviously lodged in her heart. After we determined that she was going to survive, I ever so gently reminded her that we decided before the party that there weren't going to be any tears this year.

In a somewhat coaxing yet encouraging way, I said, "Remember, you made a promise."

Reagan had made a promise to herself that if she got bumped and was not hurt, she would be OK. She'd be able to handle it. She also readily agreed that she did not want the pictures to be like the ones she had last year. Reagan wanted to be happy, and since she actually likes to have her picture taken, she wanted to be smiling. I assured her that she was going to be OK and asked her if she would please come out of the bounce house so we could go inside and sing "Happy Birthday" to her.

Without any hesitation at all, Reagan came out of the bounce house and started up the deck stairs to go back into the house. She was following me up the steps when about half way up, she stopped. I looked back at her, and I observed her very conscientiously wiping her eyes. Her crying had ceased, and she obviously did not want any hint of her tears to show. She remembered her promise, and she was going to make sure there were no signs of it being broken. As she rigorously continued to wipe her eyes, my eyes came close to welling up with tears. I was such a proud nana!

Promises are hard to keep. In fact, sometimes it is just not possible to keep them. It is the intent of the heart that God looks at and not the circumstance that causes the stumble to happen. He knows all about our motives and our ambitions and whether they are honorable or not. Our Lord is alert to and appreciative of our humanity.

This story is not about sad versus happy pictures. Admittedly, it is about my wanting my precious granddaughter to have a happy birthday with happy memories. And it is also about God's faithfulness and His promises. If her body had been hurt, the narrative would be different, but her body was not harmed. A child bumped into her, and she could choose to get over it or not. Thankfully, she elected not to let the incident ruin the day.

God promises to be faithful to us in all situations. That there will be both happy as well as hurtful occasions is a given. There are all kinds of wounds and different types of suffering. The Lord knows the feelings of a five-year-old, and they are just as important as the feelings of those who are more mature. The Lord is our Healer, Protector, and Guide, and He knows.

The Lord used me to comfort and help Reagan. And the Lord used Reagan to bless me as I watched her dry her eyes. Praise be to God!

Key Thought

God is faithful to His promises.

Scripture

"For the word of the LORD is right and true; he is faithful in all he does" (Psalm 33:4).

Prayer

Thank You, Lord, for the many different ways You demonstrate Your promise of faithfulness to us. Help us to be used to bless others. As we seek to honor You, may Your glory be revealed. Thank You for Your presence at all times, in all places and in all situations. You hear our cries, and You know our hearts and we praise You for Your faithfulness. In Christ's name we pray. Amen.

For Further Reflection

1. Do you really believe that God keeps all of His promises?

2. Do you think it is possible to keep all of the promises we make to God and to others?
3. Have you been wounded by broken promises? If so, how have you responded to the hurt?
4. How has your ability to trust been affected by your experiences with promises?

3 | Fresh Flowers

November 17, 2018

When Reagan celebrated her fifth birthday, as with all her previous birthday parties, it was a big event. Her mom always creates fantastic DIY decorations, and there is always a well thought-out and carefully designed theme. This year the theme was *My Little Pony*. We have all kinds of cute photos of Reagan dressed up standing in front of rainbows and of her holding a variety of colors of stuffed little ponies.

When I asked her what she would like for her birthday, she said she wanted flowers. When probed about what kind of flowers, she said she wanted a bunch that had lots of colors to include blue, pink, yellow, and purple. She must have been thinking about the rainbow when she was listing the colors.

Reagan has lots of toys but whenever she sees a commercial on TV about a new toy, she spontaneously informs all who will listen that she wants that toy. So it was interesting to learn that on the day that she might actually get one of those toys advertised on TV, she wanted multi-colored fresh flowers.

When I learned that Reagan wanted flowers, I bought some for her. But I didn't pay close enough attention to each color that she had listed. Mommy did, though. When Reagan received what she very specifically asked for from Mommy, she was delighted. It was obviously very important to her to have it be right!

When you think about it, flowers are in no way a true necessity. But they are a very pleasant complement to any setting. We celebrate with flowers on most holidays and certain kinds of flowers are associated with different times of the year and special occasions. Poinsettias and Christmas go together just as lilies are the flower of choice for Easter. Reagan was right that fresh flowers are special on birthdays and ones with lots of color surely reminded her of the *My Little Pony* theme.

I just think, though, that for a five-year-old child to choose flowers over toys is extraordinary. Well, of course, as we all know, Reagan is exceptional, so I would naturally think that! Something that is fresh and beautiful appeals to most of us and bouquets of flowers cheer many of us. I know several women who buy flowers each week for themselves. Why?

I think it is because we all have a yearning deep inside us for that well-spring of life that flowers so exquisitely represent. Our Creator did not have to put flowers on this earth. We probably could have gotten along without them. Yet, He did. Our Lord wants us to savor all the things that draw us to Himself. The bounty of His extravagance in nature is really far beyond our understanding. Amazingly, we have beauty to enjoy every single day! We just have to open our eyes to receive it. Not only will we see beyond the splendor, we may also experience an added touch as we draw in deeper and intentionally seek to absorb it all.

All of us, young and old, have available to us the option to dwell in the sacred spaces of nature. As we "consider the lilies", we are able not only to enjoy the present, but also have the glorious opportunity to abide in the bliss of the Divine. It is at that point one rainbow-colored bouquet takes on shades far beyond our Imagination.

Key Thought

Fresh flowers remind many of us about the wonder of creation and the Creator.

Scripture

"The earth is the LORD'S and everything in it; the world and all who live in it" (Psalm 24:1).

Prayer

Thank You, Lord, for the awesome beauty that is all around us. You are the Creator of all things and You are our All in all. May we always remember to give You the glory for Your provision. We see Your majesty in the sights, sounds, and smells of nature and we are struck by the extravagance and the abundance of it all. May we never cease to give You praise! With grateful hearts, we pray. Amen.

For Further Reflection

1. What kinds of things or activities cause you to pause, reflect, and consider the wonders of creation?
2. How can you translate question one's considerations into corresponding actions?
3. Throughout your daily routine, is it generally difficult or easy for you to maintain an attitude of praise? Give details.
4. When was the last time you gave someone fresh flowers as a random act of kindness?

4 | God Steadies the Flail in the Sail

December 4, 2018

Sometimes I don't know exactly what words I should use to describe the uneasy feeling of not knowing what to say or how to react. It is a conundrum, for sure. When I am struggling to know, sometimes all I do is flail. I feel like a swimmer in the ocean being tossed around and helpless to make any headway. Emotional thrashing about is hurtful to us and often to others.

Unfortunately, such was the case with dear Reagan when I recently went to her house for a visit. We had not seen each other for about six weeks and for me it felt like six years. For her part, she was just acting awkward. When I entered her house, she began squealing and running around in a big circle while laughing and acting shy all at the same time. Naturally I wanted her to run up to me the second she saw me and start expounding upon how much she missed me, but somehow the time we had been apart obviously made her uncomfortable.

When I managed to catch her in the loop she was making around the house, she then returned my embrace with great fervor. I had to be the one to initiate the hug but from that point forward, we were bosom buddies and back in our routine of playing games and reading books. Admittedly, that initial little hiccup of awkwardness caught me by surprise.

As our time together continued, I decided to ask her if she missed me. Again, my heart was wanting to hear that life away from her nana was hard (unbearable). But I knew better and her reply was actually quite amazing. She simply stated, "Nana, I missed all my Colorado friends and family." How mature.

Often when adults don't know what to do or say, they find activities to divert their attention off the real subject at hand. It is much easier to watch a football game than it is to talk. The precious baby or the cute puppy gets the attention. Of course, all that has its place, but too often it becomes a substitute for the real conversation that needs to happen. It is often difficult to take the first step. Those first words or gestures can feel seemingly impossible to articulate or initiate. It is simply easier to redirect focus elsewhere.

We all experience times when we find ourselves spinning around and often that happens when a major event occurs. Health issues and relational challenges have a tendency to stop us dead in our tracks and we find ourselves lost. Not knowing how to respond, we are in a quagmire; a different kind of spinning. If we are wise, we can choose to reach out to the only One who can stop our spiraling. As we abandon our gyrating, the Lord holds us, steadies us, and showers His love upon us. As in all relationships, when we focus our attention on each other, we can begin to enjoy being renewed, restored, and revitalized.

Too often, we needlessly run around in circles. The Lord's arms are always there to catch us and when we yield, just like Reagan did, we are back in the game again. It does not have to be awkward. The Lord takes the flail out of the sail!

Key Thought

God steadies the flail in the sail.

Scripture

"The LORD is my rock, my fortress and my deliverer; my God is my rock, in whom I take refuge. He is my shield and the horn of my salvation, my stronghold" (Psalm 18:2).

Prayer

Thank You, dear Heavenly Father, for being all that You say You are! Thank You that You are the only One who can steady us in the storm. You know our weaknesses and how sometimes it is difficult for us to do the right thing even when we know what we ought to do. Please help us to stop our flailing and ask for help, trusting that we will receive the direction that we need. You are our rock and our compass. Help us to place our trust in You. In the mighty name of Jesus, we pray. Amen.

For Further Reflection

1. Think about a time you were in a situation where you did not want to bring up a certain sensitive topic but you knew you needed to do so. How did you handle it and what was your reasoning for doing it that way?
2. Are you accustomed to seeking the Lord's counsel first about difficult issues? If not, what are you more often inclined to do?
3. When you have not received insight from the Lord, what has been your response?
4. Where and how do you divert your attention in order to avoid facing the real issues?

"Worrying does not empty tomorrow of its troubles, it empties today of its strength."

Corrie ten Boom

5 | "R"

December 14, 2018

Reagan, with a very serious face and eyes staring directly at me, stated, "Nana, I wrote an 'R' on your car."

I knew my car was dirty so I asked her if she wrote the "R" where it was dirty. She replied that was what she indeed had done. I laughed and said that it was OK that she did that. She smiled and then skipped away. Often, we see where someone has written "Wash me" on a dirty car. It is neither a good thing nor a bad thing when someone does that. To quote a commonly used phrase, "It just is what it is."

It strikes me that Reagan felt compelled to tell me about that action. She must have thought that *maybe* it was not right to write on my car so she felt she needed to fess up. We all experience those kinds of insecurities when we are not quite sure whether we should speak up or not. When we are unsure, there is one answer: Ask God! More often than not and frequently regardless of the consequences, we know that telling the truth is the right thing to do.

As I write this, I can hear the reader responding that there are exceptions to that statement. When withholding the truth is for honorable reasons, perhaps it is warranted. For example, when my sweet father suddenly became very ill while in the hospital and was slipping away before our eyes, we did not discuss his medical diagnosis or his prognosis with him. There was no point to do that but technically speaking, we were withholding the truth from him.

We can all think of times when we did not fully disclose information and we regretted it and other times when we knew we were correct in doing so. We can trust God to give us the discernment we need to make the tough decisions. Back to this little scenario with Reagan, I am thankful that her inner spirit prompted her to tell me what she had done. There will be many other circumstances where the issue will be much more serious and I pray that when that occurs, she will listen and she will respond with integrity.

We know that the Lord delights in those who are truthful and He promises to give us the discernment we need about how best to impart truth. We must be deliberate, cautious, and patient. He will give us the wisdom we need to speak the truth in love.

I know that Reagan wrote the "R" on my dirty car because it was the first letter of her name. But for my money, that "R" stood for <u>R</u>ight on, Reagan!

Key Thought

Tell the truth!

Scripture

"The LORD detests lying lips, but He delights in men who are truthful" (Proverbs 12:22).

Prayer

Thank You, Lord, that You know us and You promise to guide us. You know our words before we speak them. Help us patiently to seek what is right and what is true. May our words reflect Your light with all whom we encounter. Please enable us to be cautious as well as courageous with our words. We thank You for being the way, the truth, and the life. In the name of Jesus we pray. Amen.

For Further Reflection

1. When have you known that you needed to speak the whole truth about something, but didn't? What stopped you?
2. Do you think it is sometimes OK not to tell the truth? Share a personal example.
3. Have you ever been hurt by not knowing the truth about something? If so, how did you come to terms with the issue? Or, is it still unresolved?
4. How do you personally relate to the scripture that instructs us that Jesus is the way, the truth, and the life? Give examples.
5. Thank God for a sensitive conscience!

Photo by Deborah Denison Bailey, 2021

6 | Mr. Turtle

February 19, 2019

It seems like the "terrible two's" have hit at age five. Reagan wants her way and that is the end of the story as far as she is concerned.

As her mom was picking her up from a fun weekend at our house, Reagan decided that she was not going to leave without taking my very large stuffed animal that is a turtle, appropriately named, Mr. Turtle. When Reagan was small, she was terrified of Mr. Turtle. But now, she uses him to sit on as a seat when she watches TV and she drags him around the house wherever she goes. This huge, lumpy green turtle is a permanent fixture in the Bailey household and he is considered to be Reagan's property. However, he lives at my house - not hers. Mr. Turtle is always waiting for her in the den. When she arrives, they are companions until she leaves - until now.

On that particular day, Reagan was determined to take Mr. Turtle with her. A very prolonged, not so pleasant, conversation ensued between Mommy and Reagan. Reagan wanted to take Mr. Turtle home but that was not a good idea because the puppies at her house would have shredded him in the blink of an eye. As time wore on, it was obvious that Reagan was not going to yield. So, Mommy removed Mr. Turtle from Reagan's arms, plucked her up, and took her to the car. All the while, Reagan was screaming and flailing as she was buckled into her car seat and they were on their way.

The whole scene hurt my already wounded heart.

It wasn't that long ago that my darling granddaughter was agreeing with everything I said, telling me that I made her heart happy and that she would always listen to me. Times have changed quickly and rather radically. When I tried to reason with her about Mr. Turtle, she remained curled up in a ball and would not look at me.

Again, the whole scene hurt my now *bleeding* heart.

Kids grow up quickly and they form their own opinions about most things. The brief, tender, sweet time when you are the center of their world fades away so rapidly. As they are developing their own thoughts and opinions about things, often their relationships change also. Suddenly, parents and grandparents aren't as wise and too frequently the bond that seemed solid becomes frayed. Sometimes the relationship is restored and sometimes it isn't. No one is always right and no one is always wrong. Somewhere along the way there needs to be a realization of that fact. We need to be allowed to be wrong without the relationship being hurt.

There will be many other scenarios that will be a lot more dire than whether Mr. Turtle can be taken home or not. Right now the much bigger issue is about honoring each other when we disagree. Scripture has much to say about that. In Romans 12:10, we are reminded to "honor one another above yourselves." How we endeavor to do that says a lot about us and who we wish to be as well as become.

In this story with the battle about the turtle, submission to authority was the last thing Reagan wanted to do. The Bible instructs us to honor our parents and to surrender to their authority. I have to wonder how our conduct gets that message across to our children and our grandchildren. It seems to me that the very best way to set an example is first to commit to endeavoring to be steadfast in our faith walk. Our behavior reflects our values and there are lots of times that means we must say "no" to things that we really want to say "yes" to doing. We honor God when we make those difficult choices.

Reagan did not want to accept the reasonable explanation that the dogs at her house would have pulled Mr. Turtle apart and made an awful mess. Too many times we don't want to accept that the Lord's guidelines are intended for our good so that our lives don't end up in shambles. Above all, we would be wise to choose to honor the Lord as we make all our choices. When we do that, all the stuffing will stay intact for the next adventure.

Key Thought

Lay down the turtle. Be rational in laying down a concept or arguing a point. Make sense when explaining... then, stand your ground!

Scripture

"Honor one another above yourselves" (Romans 12:10).

Heavenly Lord, thank You for your Word that guides us. Help us to listen carefully when You instruct us to honor our parents and others. Help us to remember that when we heed Your commands, we are honoring You. Forgive us when we fuss and fight to have our own way. Help us to remember that our relationship with You and with others is more important than our wants. We need Your Light to guide us and we trust that You will provide all the illumination we need to honor You as we make our decisions. Thank You for loving us, knowing us, and guiding us. In Your holy name we pray. Amen.

For Further Reflection

1. How often do your wants guide your decisions?
2. Do you trust that the Lord knows what is best for you? If so, how do you demonstrate that?
3. Have you had to sacrifice your needs or wants for the sake of honoring a valued relationship? Explain.
4. In what ways do you honor others above yourself?

Reagan's Mr. Turtle
Photo by Deborah Denison Bailey, 2020

7 | Just Say I'm Six

February 23, 2019

Reagan, Bampa and I enjoy the wonderful blessing of being members of an athletic spa and club. What we relish most is the warm therapy pool and the pool area for kids which has three sizes of slides and an array of water fountains. We often go on Friday evenings and it is always fun.

There is also a wonderful outdoor hot tub there. Recently, I asked Reagan if she would mind sitting on the side and waiting for me while I went in the hot tub. I had never done that before with her. You have to be at least six years old to be allowed to get in the hot tub. Since she is five and I can't leave her unattended, I was hoping that my little indulgent request would be agreeably met. It was.

As I was delighting in the steamy water and she was watching me, she asked why she had to be six to be able to go in the hot water. I explained to her that it was too hot and at her age, it could hurt her heart. She became much more interested in trying to find a way around the rule about age. Her idea was that if the lifeguard came by and asked how old she was, she would just say she was six.

That response did not surprise me much but I tried to explain to her that we should never lie and that telling the truth was always the best thing to do. There is a difference between lying and not telling the truth. There was no lifeguard around the area that evening and no one would have known the difference if she had gone in the hot tub. Of course, we would have known.

Again, we don't necessarily need to lie to be untruthful. We can all list many different situations when this is true. For example, we might get too much change back at the grocery store and just pocket it rather than return it. And what about taxes? Are we inclined to try to change the numbers a little for our benefit? We might be convicted by our conscience, the Holy Spirit or simply guilt. Whatever it is, I think it is important to listen to that inner voice and ask God as well as thank God for the courage to tell the truth.

As Reagan and I were leaving, we asked the receptionist at the front desk if kids were allowed to dangle their feet in the hot tub if they weren't six yet. Nope. That was not allowed either. Actually, the way the lady explained the reason was very kind, yet firm. She did quite a good job but the "ears to hear" weren't quite there.

The following Friday, Reagan did sit on the edge of the hot tub while I went in for a few minutes. She did not put her feet in but she did have a little mermaid doll with her and the tail of that toy managed to slip into the water. I guess her dolly was six.

Key Thought

Tell the truth.

Scripture

"These are the things you are to do: Speak the truth to each other" (Zechariah 8:16a).

Prayer

Dear Heavenly Lord, thank You for being the way, the truth, and the life. We earnestly ask for help to find our way as we seek You in truth. We know that we are instructed to seek righteousness to speak truth. You know how hard it can be for us, but You also offer us the way. Because of You, we can find the courage to seek, find, and speak truth. After all, You are Truth. We praise and thank You. In Your holy name we pray. Amen.

For Further Reflection

1. When is it OK not to tell the whole truth? Give an example.
2. How do you know when the Holy Spirit is convicting you? Explain.
3. Name a time when a lie backfired. What did you learn from that experience?
4. Give a personal example of when you withheld the truth for honorable reasons. What was the outcome?
5. What about merely shades of truth?

"Half a truth is often a great lie."

Benjamin Franklin

8 | Ouch!

March 9, 2019

Reagan and I often sit down at my piano together and sing songs. I play the songs and she carefully situates her little fingers on the keys in quite a deliberate way and seems to think that she is actually playing the right melody with me. It is a lovely experience and even if the product is not at all musically accurate, our hearts are singing.

On this particular day, Reagan requested a song called, "Down in My Heart". That was one that we learned a long time ago together. She remembers the chorus that repeatedly says "I'm so happy. I've got the love of Jesus in my heart." When I reminded her about the verses, she became a little less engaged. One of the verses says, "And if the devil doesn't like it, he can sit on a tack." I wondered if she understood the words that she was singing. So, I asked her. "Reagan, do you know what a tack is?"

"No."

After I explained to her what a tack was, I asked, "Reagan, do you know who the devil is?"

Again, she replied, "No."

When I told her that the devil was bad, she asked me

the best question of all. "Nana, you mean you want to hurt him?"

Hmm.

"Reagan, the lyrics in the song do want the devil to sit on something sharp and be hurt." I then thought and rather falteringly said, "But maybe Jesus would like the devil to be good and not be hurt." The simple truth is, however, that the devil is not a person and should not be treated as one.

There are lots of people who do very bad things and we call them bad people. Are they really terrible people? More often than not, we want bad things to happen to those people whose actions we judge are bad. If we have the "love of Jesus in our hearts" as the lyrics say, then should our happy hearts want something bad to happen to the people we consider to be bad? Is that what we would then call justice?

This little five-year-old child has stopped me dead in my tracks today. I am thinking that if justice results in discipline then the person being disciplined may feel hurt by it, but the intent is for good. Simply said, the hurt may happen, but the action is based upon a desire for well-being. In other words, it is "tough love". Whew! For a kid's song, that may be way too heavy an analysis! But we all know that very often when we cry for justice, it is not sought because we want the best for a person. We want that tack to hurt! Badly.

If we are happy as we experience our daily walks through our lives and the reason really is because we have the love of Jesus in our hearts, we should want the best for others. As we instruct children, how thoughtfully do we discipline them and still get the message across that we love them? When we disagree or are literally injured by others, how do we convey that our love for Jesus dictates our responses? Too often, our own hurts rule and add momentum to the cycle of hurts.

We are tested all the time. Do our lives demonstrate our love for Jesus or are we more consumed with sharpening the tack for our oppressors to sit upon? If we resonate more with the latter option, hear the Lord saying, "Ouch!" now. We would all do well to question some of our reasoning and actions that resulted in others being hurt. As we do so, we might realize that the outcomes may have been different if we had truly sought the Lord's counsel. We might even decide that we should have been the one sitting on that tack. Ouch!

Key Thought

May the love of Jesus govern all our thoughts and actions.

Scripture

"Dear children, let us not love with words or tongue but with actions and in truth" (1 John 3).

Prayer

Heavenly Father, thank You for the call for introspection today. Thank You for Reagan's piercing words which revealed so many layers for potential thought that we hardly know where to begin to start peeling them off. We trust that You have a message for each of us. We confess that many of our actions have been made in haste and were results of fear and hurt. Help us to strive to want the best for those who have harmed us. We know that You want the best for all of Your children. We wish to honor You with our conduct and we bow down to You and give You all the honor, glory, and praise. You are our Savior and the devil has no power over us unless we let him. Protect us, guide us, and please help us to address difficult issues and see them through Your eyes. We love You. In Christ's name we pray. Amen.

For Further Reflection

1. What would you have said to Reagan concerning the devil sitting on a tack? Cite scripture that supports your reasoning.
2. Does your daily conduct reflect your love for Jesus? Give specific examples.
3. Whom would you like to sit on a tack? Do you feel justified to want that?
4. Another interesting aspect of this story is that my granddaughter had never heard of the devil. How do you think young children should be told about the devil? Explain in detail.

> *"You, dear children, are from God and have overcome them because the One who is in you is greater than the one who is in this world" (1John 4:4).*

9 | Ouch! - Part II

March 10, 2019

I am still hurting from the visual image in my mind of Reagan's face when she said, "You mean you want to hurt him (the devil)?" I think there were several different directions I could have written about yesterday. Today, I would like to take another route.

I don't know why I was surprised that Reagan had never heard of the devil. Truth be told, throughout my childhood, I never remember hearing about him. In fact, even though I have attended church all my life, I do not remember talk about the Holy Spirit, either. That is all very unfortunate and, sadly there are many others like me who also grew up in churches where they experienced these omissions.

I mostly remember hearing that Jesus loved me and that He had forgiven my sins. That is wonderful and that is good to know. But in all my years of singing professionally or leading music in many different churches, I failed to hear the rest of the story. I still wonder how that happened.

When I was in my forties, a very wise woman asked me if I thought people were good? After a lot of thought, I replied that I thought people were sinful and living in a broken world. I remember thinking that she would try to dissuade my opinion because I thought my reply was extremely radical. Instead, she told me I was right and from that time forward, I have been soaking in all I can learn, to include knowledge about, as well as communing with, the Holy Spirit. Again, I wonder how I could have been so clueless since I spent so much time in church. I even attended a Christian secondary boarding school! Ouch!

As I think about Reagan and remember the curious and perplexed look on her face, I know that the Lord is still prompting me to come up with some answers for her. So, how do you address the subject of the devil with a five-year-old child? We know the devil is an enemy of God and we know that he will end up in the lake of fire eventually. Until then, we are instructed to know that God can't be tempted by evil. Nothing about God is evil. When we put on the full armor of God, we are protected.

When we recite the "Lord's Prayer", we say "lead us not into temptation, but deliver us from the evil one (Matt 6:13)." Children hear the "Lord's Prayer" and they hear the word, "evil". If we say that the evil one is bad, kids should be able to relate to that. Further, when we are tempted to do something bad, we can trust that if we think about what Jesus would do in that circumstance, we just might not do that bad thing.

How do you teach a child to resist temptation when adults don't do a very good job of it? Scripture clearly tells us, "Resist the devil and he will flee from you," (James

4:7b). Additionally, "Come near to God and He will come near to you," (James 4:8). Those are great references but how do you enable and equip young ears to hear the message? Again, perhaps I was exposed to that passage about the devil in Sunday School, but I certainly have no memory of it. Using relatable language and endeavoring not to avoid the topic are keys.

I am still bothered by, "You mean you want to hurt him (the devil)?" Somehow, I think we need to get across the message that God will deal with the devil. Both God and we have roles. But yes, I do want to "hurt" the devil by resisting and shunning, etc. That is an important personal role. I want to tell Reagan and all the other children that when we have a feeling that something is wrong or bad, we need to follow those instincts. When we resist doing that "bad" thing, we are honoring our Savior. Fighting the attack of the devil is a lifelong endeavor. It takes lots of commitment, persistence, and often it is a difficult choice. Only with Jesus is it possible to refuse to go along with all the things the devil tries to manipulate us into doing. His Holy Spirit enables us to repel the attack and to endure the struggle.

We are victors through Christ whose armor we are offered. We honor Him when we pray, read His Word, and take time to try to instruct, support, and encourage others. With the wisdom that only God can provide, we can help raise up a new generation of informed, strong, fully-armored young men and women of God! If we choose to shirk that responsibility and listen to that other voice, there's a tack being sharpened for us and it is only a matter of time before we end up sitting on it. Ouch!

Key Thought

God will deal with the devil and our very significant role is to resist him.

Scripture

"Resist the devil and he will flee from you" (James 4:7b).

Prayer

Thank You, dear Heavenly Lord, for being our Almighty God! You are all powerful and all-knowing with plans both for us and for the devil. Help us to equip ourselves with Your full armor. Hear our hearts as we earnestly pray for Your wisdom. Help us to trust You and Your timing as we teach the young. We thank You for the mentors in our lives who help us navigate through life's tough questions. Your provision supplies our need and we give You the glory for that. In the holy name of Jesus we pray. Amen.

For Further Reflection

1. Do you think that young children should be taught about the devil? Why or why not?
2. What did you learn about the devil when you were young and how have you grown in your knowledge about him? Or not?

3. When you know something is bad, do you think it is your conscience or the Holy Spirit speaking to you? How do you know the difference? Explain.
4. If you were teaching a five-year-old child about the devil, what are some of the words you would choose?

"I do not understand what I do. For what I want to do I do not do, but what I hate to do" (Romans 7:15).

"For I have the desire to do what is good, but I cannot carry it out. For what I do is not the good I want to do; no, the evil I do not want to do – this I keep on doing" (Romans 18b – 19).

Devil Sitting on a Thumbtack

Drawing by Megan Denison Smith, 2021

10 | A Little Streppy

March 27, 2019

Reagan seems to be prone to getting strep throat a lot. She is absolutely fine one day and the next day her throat is raging and she is positive for strep. Needless to say, this on-going affliction is a source of concern and it has caused us to postpone some weekend plans.

Today when Bampa and I picked Reagan up from daycare, we asked her how she was feeling. We knew she had just gone through another bout with strep. She had been on antibiotics for a week and seemed to be back into her normal routine. Her reply was cute: "I'm just a little streppy." We thought that response was adorable and we then proceeded to enjoy a fun time at an outdoor playground.

Reagan could have told us that she was just fine but she chose to remind us of her recent malady. Many people opt to make that same choice. We often find ourselves enduring a long diatribe about ailments when we ask how someone is doing. Too frequently we hear more information and details than we desire to know. I wonder why we do that? Why do we become more absorbed in telling folks about our troubles rather than our good fortunes? We are bombarded daily in the news with all the minutia of all the bad stuff because that is what sells.

Wouldn't it be something if there were news services that offered *only* good news? I know that is not an original query but can you imagine multiple networks competing to tell happy stories? I have to wonder how long they would stay in business. It is a shame that more attention is not given to all the good that is happening all the time. When there is a special report about an extraordinary happening, it is often presented as though it is highly unusual: a miracle.

Rather than allow ourselves to be drawn to the negative, we would be wise to highlight all the good news there is every chance we get. The bottom line is that Jesus is our good news! As we open our eyes to all the wonder that life has to offer, we are empowered to see the silver linings even in the things that are troublesome. Scripture reminds us we can trust that God knows the plans for us and they are to prosper us and not to harm us. Even when things are a little "streppy", Jesus has the answer for all life's challenges so that we can literally live well and prosper!

Key Thought

Jesus is our good news!

Scripture

"'For I know the plans I have for you,' declares the LORD, 'plans to prosper you and not to harm you, plans to give you hope and a future'" (Jeremiah 29:11).

Prayer

Heavenly Lord, it is so amazing that You knew all about us before we were even born. Help us to remember that Your sovereignty reigns over all things great and small. Nothing is a surprise to You! Help us to show You our gratitude for Your plans for our lives, even when we don't understand our circumstances. We praise and honor You through our tears. We thank You for Your provision for our lives. We are so grateful and we pray all these things in the mighty name of Jesus. Amen.

For Further Reflection

1. Is your glass half empty or half full? Explain your answer.
2. Name the people in your life who have been positive influences for you? Specifically share the impact they have had upon you and thank God for them.
3. How do you answer the question, "Why do bad things happen to good people?"
4. In what ways has the Lord demonstrated His plans to prosper you?

11 | T - R - Y - I - N - G to Try

April 22, 2019

Once again, Reagan is battling her urge to be shy. Thankfully, adults who know her are kind and understanding when she yields to the desire not to respond. If there was a physical manifestation of what happens when she "freezes," it would look like a solid steel cage descending down over her entire body with not even a peep hole to provide for any curiosity. This totally frozen state is dark and scary. She remains in this pose until the threat of the encounter ends and then in a flash, she merrily transforms back into the happy-go-lucky kid that she is and the world is rosy again.

Reagan and I often talk about her shyness. She readily admits that she does not know why she gets this way. I frequently ask her to try to talk with my adult friends when we are with them. Sometimes our talking before meeting them has helped. She tells me she wants to overcome her fear and she doesn't understand it. Recently she has been able to muster the courage at least to do a high five and that has seemed to build her confidence a bit. She also waves to people and appears to enjoy doing that.

In a very genuine and almost agonizing way, Reagan told me she was trying to speak to others. When I asked her how she was trying, she gave me a very good answer: "Nana, I am trying to try."

That's the preparation before the action: the pep-talk before the game. As I listened to her reply, my heart, which I thought couldn't love her more than it already does, found another way to expand – totally overflowing with the absolute joy of adoring her.

"Trying to try" is a pretty deep concept. As we search for ways to deal with conflicts that baffle, disarm, and even scare us, we would do well to try to confront the big challenges by summoning the courage to take the first step of "trying to try."

How do we help a youngster do this when as adults we often become stymied by our own struggles? For the believer, Christ is our answer. It should be a natural reflex, but often it is not. The enemy loves to sidetrack us with all kinds of diversions. Sadly, many times when we take alternate routes, we get so off-course that we fail to find the right direction again.

In John 14:6, Jesus tells us, "I am the way and the truth, and the life." I wonder why we try to complicate that so much. Perhaps it is a trust issue. To further complicate matters, there are so many other voices competing for attention. Actually, I think that might be what is going on with Reagan. She knows that her adult friends are caring and loving but there is another voice inside her vying for her consideration. We all experience frequent skirmishes like that. We wrestle in different and unique ways. How often do we try asking God as our first line of defense?

Every chance I get, I plan to try to comfort Reagan by telling her we all have struggles and that how to respond to them can often be very hard. In fact, it is normal to feel uncomfortable and she is not alone. Unfortunately, not everyone knows that the Lord can do battle with us to ward off those other voices. Jesus is the good news for every situation and we don't have to try so hard because He is with us and He is for us. The very best way to "try to try" is to give the battle to Jesus. That dark place will then become illuminated by His light, His way, and His truth.

Key Thought

"Trying to try" is a wise first step.

Scripture

"Jesus answered, 'I am the way and the truth, and the life'" (John 14:6).

Prayer

Thank You, Lord Jesus, that when we bring our petitions to You, You hear us and use us for Your good purpose. Thank You that You understand our trials. You never leave us nor forsake us. You understand our pain and we ask You to help us feel Your loving arms around us in a powerful and mighty way. Help us to come to You with our struggles and to lean on You to provide the courage we need to bravely face our troubles. We give You the glory for our victory and we pray these things in the powerful name of Jesus. Amen.

For Further Reflection

1. Can you relate to the phrase, "trying to try"? Explain.
2. What are some diversions that you allow which prevent you from going to Jesus first?
3. Put into your own words what it means to you when Jesus says that He is the way.
4. Share a time when Jesus rescued you from a very difficult situation. Now give Him the glory!

"Silver is purified in fire and so are we. It is in the most trying times that our real character is shaped and revealed."

Helen Keller
QUOTEFANCY

12 | Not Just a Chevy

May 29, 2019

Reagan has a keen eye for spotting the many different brands of cars on the road. Specifically, she can spot the models and makes of cars that her family drives: Ford (Mustang), Hummer, and Chevrolet. With pride and glee she pipes up with, "There's a Hummer like my Daddy's" or "There's a Chevy like my Mommy's car." It is a fun, engaging game we frequently play while riding in the car.

As we were cruising along one day, we spotted a Chevy. Coincidentally, Mommy and I both drive a Chevrolet Equinox. Reagan immediately recognizes it and likes to tell me every single time that both Mommy and I have the same brand and model of car. During this particular outing, she explained to me that she knew that there were different models but they were all Chevys because of the symbol. It was at that point that she paused and very thoughtfully said, "You know, Nana, if you put the car on its side, then the Chevy symbol would look like a Jesus cross."

Wow! I loved that!

Many people see God everywhere: His handprint is on everything. Things in nature often elicit responses from people about the beauty of the world which the Lord created. Even when things do not appear so beautiful, there are many people who still see His handiwork and say things like, "The Lord is teaching me a lesson right now. I have no idea what it is, but I trust that, in His good time, I will."

Reagan was right. There are signs of the cross everywhere!

Key Thought

God IS everywhere!

Scripture

"The earth is the Lord's and everything in it, the world, and all who live in it" (Psalm 24).

Prayer

Thank You, Lord, for Your presence! You are everywhere at all times and we are so grateful to know that You are always with us. We give You praise for all that You are and we wish to honor You by giving You the glory You deserve at all times. Please help us to see the cross in our every circumstance and to remember the price You paid for us all. May we always keep our eyes on the cross! In Your holy name we pray. Amen.

For Further Reflection

1. How do you endeavor to keep your eyes on the cross? Be very specific as you answer.
2. Explain some ways that the Lord has reminded you that He is sovereign over all things in your life.
3. How do you explain things that happen which you know are contrary to the Lord's will?
4. When was the last time the Lord revealed Himself to you in a strong and mighty way? What was your response?

13 | Down Under

August 3, 2019

One of the activities we enjoy most is going to the pool together. Since Reagan was very young, she has always wanted to go to a place we call Villa. She especially loves going down the slides. Now that she is almost six, we decided together that it was about time for her to learn how to swim. She's been working very hard on that skill and has been especially concentrating on learning how to hold her breath while submerged.

Very proudly and confidently, Reagan will practice this task by holding her nose and briefly going underwater and then bouncing back up. Each time she surfaces, she holds both arms up and exclaims, "I did it!" Going underwater was a big milestone. The length of time down under varies from brief to very brief. It is nonetheless a major accomplishment and we all revel in her success and progress.

Recently we encountered a mom who was throwing in the water a missile-like rubber toy which proceeded to travel to the bottom of the pool. Her son then quickly dove down to catch the missile before it reached the bottom, which was about three feet deep.

When Reagan saw that, she immediately went over to the mom and boy and asked if she could play with them. Who could get to that toy first? That was the catalyst that made Reagan forget about holding her nose and thinking about how long she was underwater. Suddenly the mission was to see who could retrieve the toy first. Without even thinking about it, she was like a little frog making her way underwater to get that toy! Reagan made a gargantuan leap in improvement when the competitive bug bit! Wow! She had a great time and she was swimming underwater like she had always done it! Amazing!

I could hardly believe my eyes as I watched her diving down and swimming like she actually knew what she was doing! It was mesmerizing to observe her glee as well as her success! The mom could not have been more accommodating either. What fun!

As I shared this success story with Reagan's mom, she rather amusingly replied, "I wonder whom she got that competitiveness from?" She was not so subtly referring to me! Unfortunately, my desire to win has not always been considered to be my most admirable trait!

In this instance, Reagan's desire to get to the toy first enabled her to improve her swimming skills without even thinking about it. Her desire to win was helpful for her progress. Reagan's confidence in the water grew because of her desire to succeed. Even though she was not the first one to get to the toy first very often, she had a blast trying to.

A wise friend of mine reminded me that just as Reagan asked the mother if she could join in with her son in the pool game, Jesus also asks us to make our requests known. We are to come "boldly to the throne of grace" (Hebrews 4:16). God hears our prayers and He expects us to join Him in fulfilling our request. After Reagan received permission to join the game, she was literally all in and relished her success in getting the toy first. That is exactly what God wants for us: the total thrill of receiving what we have asked for and the pure joy of abandoning ourselves to the task as God faithfully helps us to win! In the end, we actually receive the prize that our Lord intended for us all along!

Key Thought

Boldly ask God for the desires of your heart!

Scripture

"Come boldly to the throne of grace" (Hebrews 4:16).

Prayer

Thank You, Lord, that You always want the best for us. You answer our prayers in ways that bless us beyond our understanding. Help us to be bold as we come before Your throne of grace. And please help us to seek Your will. We long to hear Your voice clearly. We give You the glory for always knowing what is best for us. We praise You for your marvelous works in us and around us! In Christ's name we pray. Amen.

For Further Reflection

1. What is your definition of boldness?
2. What areas are easier than others completely to surrender to God?
3. Is winning important to you? Explain.
4. How challenging is it for you to "come boldly to the throne of grace"?
5. How do you deal with your failures (degrees of) and your corresponding efforts to correct them?

Playing in the Pool with New Friends
Drawing by Reagan Bailey, 2020

14 | Fursday

August 23, 2019

With a very disturbed voice, Reagan informed me that "Some kids say *Fursday*, but that is not right. You are supposed to put your tongue between your teeth and say *Thursday*." In a very serious tone, she continued on to say, "Nana, they are listening to the devil and he is telling them to say it wrong."

Hmm. How do I explain to her that even though the kids are not pronouncing the word correctly, the devil is not involved in this scenario? The difference between right and wrong in this context is different. I am thankful that she knows whom she needs to listen to. She really hasn't learned to read yet, but she already has a strong impression about His Word in her heart.

Too often, many of us are quite unsure of which voice it is we think we are hearing. Being able to discern is often very difficult. Not always specific are the God whispers and nudges – but sometimes they are! A wise choice is always to open the Word of God and our Savior will be faithful to meet us. How God's Word is presented is often a huge factor in learning right and wrong. Our backgrounds often make a big difference. With age and maturity comes change in manners, attitudes and words. There really is no excuse for *the devil made me do it* mentality when we earnestly seek the Lord's will. We can depend upon this absolute truth every day of the week, whether we pronounce the days of the week correctly or not.

Key Thought

God's word teaches us what is right and what is wrong.

Scripture

"I have hidden your word in my heart that I might not sin against you" (Psalm 119:11).

Prayer

Thank You, Lord, for giving us Your Word. Please help us to live in accordance with Your will and equip us with a discerning spirit. Guide us and fill us with Your Spirit so that all of our thoughts, words, and actions bring glory to You. In Christ's name we pray. Amen.

For Further Reflection

1. Contrast the carnal mind with the spiritual, the mind of Christ.
2. Do you search the scriptures for answers? If so, what is your method?

3. How would you have explained to Reagan the difference between right and wrong in this scenario?
4. Share specific scriptures which equip and enable you to pursue the Lord's will.

Reagan's To Do List for **thursDay**

1. scool
2. teeth
3. hair
4. klose
5. werk
6. play
7. tv
8. bicke
9. Frends
10. tether boll

Reagan's Thursday Schedule
by Reagan M. Bailey, 2019

15 | Really Hard

October 16, 2019

Reagan and I often have very engaged conversations while we are in my bedroom, away from other distractions in the rest of the house. There is no big screen TV and there is no opportunity to be lured to the back porch, another favorite spot, which is located right outside our kitchen. My room is our special place for one-on-one time, where Reagan and I snuggle on the bed and just talk.

On this particular day, I started a conversation about how fortunate she was to have such a good life, filled with fun. I started to mention some things that we had just done and as I was doing so, she interrupted me. And with a theatrical gesture, she raised her arms up and as she was dramatically flopping them back down, she emphatically stated, "Yes. But Nana, life is still just really hard!" This response was totally out of the blue and I was at a loss about how to respond. She followed up by saying, "You have to make masks."

Masks. OK, now I was beginning to understand. Halloween was right around the corner.

Reagan then proceeded to look around the room

and gather more examples to make her point. She listed things that she saw in the room: a chair, a wastebasket, an assortment of jewelry, clothes, etc. Everything that she saw, she added to her list of things that were hard to make. Reagan placed listed making a mask first on her growing list of hard things because she was thinking about Halloween!

Masks, masks. I am thinking about the masks that people wear during the day. There's the mask that hides fear and there's the one that looks happy but is really a disguise for a totally different state of mind. The list of different masks that people wear is extensive. Sometimes we wear masks for so long that we believe that that face is really who we are.

Our Savior is the only One who knows our hearts and can transform us into *being* the person He created us to be. He can help us to have the desire to remove the façade and embrace all that He intended for us. Often that process requires deep introspection – an honesty that is difficult, but always necessary. As we seek His face and strive to follow His commands, we are set free. The freedom we find in Christ enables us to honor all that we were created to be.

Reagan thinks that making a Halloween mask qualifies her belief that life is really hard. From the perspective of a six year old, I suppose that is understandable. For a child, learning to lace up and tie shoes is hardship. Having to obey and to put away toys is hardship. I just hope that as she matures, she will have the wisdom to know that wearing a false mask through life is much, much harder. I pray that she will choose to wear a mask only one time during the year and that will be only at Halloween. The rest of the time, I am going to trust that the light of Christ will be the countenance on her face.

Key Thought

May the light of Christ be what we see on our faces.

Scripture

"In the same way, let your light shine before men, that they may see your good deeds and praise your Father in heaven"(Matthew 5:16).

Prayer

Thank You, Lord, that we have You to be our guide. We praise You and thank You for Your living Word. Help us to follow Your commands so that our actions are pleasing in Your sight. Thank you that our identity is found in You alone. How awesome it is to know that You created us as unique individuals. You know us and You love us! It is our desire to honor You and be Your light for others to see. In Your holy name we pray. Amen.

For Further Reflection

1. Do you intentionally wear a mask around certain people? If you do, why?

2. Do you think it is sometimes appropriate to wear a mask around others? If so, how does it benefit them?
3. How would you have responded to a six-year-old child telling you that "life is just really hard"?
4. Describe someone you know who radiates the countenance of Christ.

This Little Light of Mine

Chorus - This little light of mine,
I'm gonna let it shine.
This little light of mine,
I'm gonna let it shine.
This little light of mine,
I'm gonna let it shine.
Let it shine, let it shine, let it shine!
Verse 1 - Hide it under a bushel, No!
I'm gonna let it shine! (Repeat x2)
Let it shine, let it shine, let it shine!
Verse 2 - Won't let Satan blow it out,
I'm gonna let it shine (Repeat x2)
Let it shine, let it shine, let it shine!

Harry Dixon Loes, Public Domain

16 | S-T-R-E-S-S-E-D OUT!

November 23, 2019

Bampa and I have a blood pressure cuff sitting on a desk. When we feel the need to check our BP, it is readily accessible. When Reagan saw it sitting there, she was prompted to make the comment, "My blood pressure is too high."

Naturally, I asked, "Why do you think it is too high, Reagan?"

"Because I am stressed out."

"Stressed out? Why are you stressed out?"

With a rather perplexed look, she replied, "I don't know."

These comments made me a little more curious so I asked, "Reagan, do you know what *stressed out* means?"

"No."

She knew the words but had no idea what they meant. I did observe, however, that she figured out that blood pressure and stress were related. That is very interesting to me. Reagan had just informed me about how hard life was and now she is telling me that she is stressed out. My, my. Is there something herein to explore! A correlation? If there is, what can I do to make sure this does not turn into something hurtful or harmful?

Lots of us have many warning signs when challenging events in our lives are about to surface. Sometimes we can truly be blindsided. It seems that more often we decide to ignore some indicators. Whether we consciously or subconsciously choose not to pay attention, that does not stop the inevitable. Even with a vague awareness that a storm is on the horizon, we tend to "reason": why go to meet it before it arrives? Right? Inertia sets in. Handling complicated situations can be very tricky.

Curiously, even when we truly do feel stressed, some of us can become lazy and comfortable in that state! At least we are familiar with the proverbial enemy. Some may even get stuck and stay in that place. That is a very sad and regrettable outcome and we probably know people who literally waste their lives away that way – stuck.

In Reagan's case, she had no idea what she was saying but she had heard it somewhere and it was attractive enough to warrant repeating. Others may use the phrase as a convenient excuse. Over time, it runs the risk of becoming a reality.

The truth is that things can be done to address blood pressure and stress. We honor ourselves and our Maker when we decide to do something about issues that make us anxious. The Lord Jesus Christ came to this earth to carry our burdens and He went to the cross for our transgressions. He has paid the full price for our every circumstance. If we believe that, then let the healing process begin! In Christ we can enjoy life to the fullest by facing our stressors with the assurance that God is with us.

We can choose to trust that the Lord will see us through, even when we really are stressed out!

Key Thought

Jesus promises to carry all our burdens.

Scripture

"Come to me all you who are weary and burdened and I will give you rest" (Matthew 11:28).

Prayer

Thanks be to You, O Lord, for being our resting place. In You, we can find refuge from the storms that rage within us. We need Your protection from all things that take our eyes off You. Sometimes it is so hard not to get tangled up in all the things that compete for our attention. Help us to know when to engage and when to walk away. We trust that You will help us choose the correct path. Thank You for carrying our burdens. Please help us seek the place of true rest which is only found in You. Amen.

For Further Reflection

1. What kinds of things stress you out?
2. When you feel overly burdened, what do you do to find relief?
3. What scriptures come to your mind that bring you comfort?
4. Do you actively try to avoid becoming stressed out? How?

"Worrying does not take away tomorrow's troubles, it takes away today's peace."

Anonymous

17 | Wow! A Unicorn!

December 14, 2019

Our outing with Reagan to see Santa was absolutely great this year. Once again, she did not want to go alone to sit on his lap. However, as she watched the other kids go see him by themselves, she mustered up her courage and trekked on up to the jolly old fellow. Her body language indicated that she was afraid but she pushed through the fear. I am not sure she even answered Santa when he asked her what she wanted for Christmas. It was enough just to go up to him by herself.

After an ever so brief exchange with Santa, his elf helper pulled an adorable cuddly stuffed animal unicorn out of his bag of toys. NOTHING, ABSOLUTELY NOTHING could have pleased Reagan more! Instantly her shriveled posture was replaced with absolute glee. With eyes wide open and a huge smile on her face, she bounced off Santa's lap and skipped back exclaiming, "Can you believe it! A unicorn! I got a unicorn!"

Bampa and I could hardly contain ourselves either. It was the perfect gift for Reagan. Absolutely perfect! Reagan routinely wore unicorn headbands and unicorn apparel. To say that she loved unicorns would be an under-statement.

Brimming with delight, she marched over to the cookie table and started telling the hostess there how happy she was to have her beautiful unicorn. She indulged Bampa and me as we took lots of pictures of her, recording her exuberance for posterity. This was a very major event. How could Santa have known the perfect gift for her?

Of course, Santa did not know. Reagan basically lucked out getting the unicorn. Or could the Holy Spirit have whispered in his ear and guided him? The fact that she was so fortunate and gleeful will probably influence how she responds to Santa the next time she goes to see him. We can only hope!

Sometimes we view God the same way. When we receive what we ask for, we are more inclined to ask again. When our expectation is not met, often our response is disappointment. Sometimes we become reluctant to keep on asking. Deep down, we may question why we should even bother. After all, unanswered prayer is depressing and gets old really fast.

Then again, unanswered prayer may be the answer – just not the one we want. During times like these, we need to remember that the Lord wants us to stay in relationship with Him. He wants to hear our hearts even when we don't have the words.

Reagan did not have the words but she did muster her courage to sit on Santa's lap. We need to do the same thing. As we sit at the throne of grace, we can be assured that our Heavenly Father will bless us with His love for us. We must commit to keep coming back, even when we don't feel like it. In His time, we will experience the "Wow" factor, also. Perhaps when we least expect it, our "unicorn" will appear and delight us, too!

Key Thought

God has the perfect gift planned for you.

Scripture

"'For I know the plans I have for you,' declares the Lord, 'plans to prosper you and not to harm you, plans to give you hope and a future'" (Jeremiah 29:11).

Prayer

It seems that when we least expect it, we receive the perfect gift from You! Thank You, Lord, for knowing us and showering us with blessings beyond our imagination and understanding. We also thank You for forgiving us when we entertain the idea that You are not listening and must not care about our concerns. Please, Lord, help us to trust You in all situations. Thank You for the perfect gift for Reagan! Santa and his elf must have had a little inside help from You! We praise You for all things great and small. In the name of Jesus we pray. Amen.

For Further Reflection

1. What is the "unicorn" that you have been praying for and what has been the Lord's response?
2. How well do you handle waiting?
3. Do you totally trust that the Lord has plans to prosper you? If so, how do you explain that to others?
4. Reflect upon a time when the Lord absolutely blessed you beyond all expectation.

A UNICORN!
The Perfect Gift from Santa!
December 2019
Photo by Deborah Denison Bailey, 2019

Santa Delivering Presents
Drawing by Reagan M. Bailey, 2019
Photo by Deborah Denison Bailey, 2019

18 | A One-Two Punch

March 20, 2020

Recently Reagan was very eager to tell me some very disturbing information. It was clear that she wanted me to share her unhappiness. We sat down together and she very angrily stated, "A big boy punched me in the belly."

Now there had to be more to the story so I probed a little more by asking, "Why did he do that to you, Reagan?"

"Well, I accidently kicked him when I was hanging on the jungle bars," she sheepishly replied. Hurriedly, she followed up by explaining, "But it was an accident that I kicked him." She very clearly emphasized that her kick was an accident. His punch was intentional.

I then asked her if she cried. Yes, she did. She also told the teacher who then instructed both of them to say that they were sorry. I was not quite sure how to comfort her when she emphatically stated, "He said he was sorry but, Nana, he didn't mean it!"

Hmm. That was the real punch in the gut.

How many times have we done the exact same thing? We say we are sorry for a wide variety of reasons. We may not want things to escalate or we possibly just want quickly to resolve the issue to keep peace. Whatever the reason, we don't really mean what we are saying. We are not sorry.

Is there a greater good to be obtained by those words? Is it better to succumb to being untruthful or insincere than to prolong an upsetting situation? In Reagan's circumstance, she was left with hurt feelings but they did continue playing on the playground – just not with each other.

This can be a tough question for many and one that we all grapple with in varying degrees. Sometimes it is truly wise to cut things off before they get ugly. As we encounter difficult situations, we all are faced with choosing our battles. Some make wiser choices than others. It is a lifetime skill that is not easily acquired – if ever.

I wonder if, when asking the Lord to forgive us, we are always remorseful. We may find ourselves unable truly to repent of whatever wrongdoing for which we seek forgiveness. We might be sorry but our behavior does not change.

We may not be sorry. To be told to say the word "sorry", apart from a little "discussion" is wrong-headed. Words can be empty and the process becomes rote only...and continues throughout life. This applies not only to children and their misbehaviors. It is a silly, vacuous, lazy way to handle a problem – for all of us.

I regret that Reagan had her feelings hurt and that the boy's apology was insincere. I am proud that she recognized it for what it was and still managed to keep playing on the playground. Now that was a wise choice.

Key Thought

Matters of the heart matter.

Scripture

"For if you forgive men when they sin against you, your heavenly Father will also forgive you" (Matthew 6:14).

Prayer

We are so grateful, Lord, that You created us and You know our hearts. Please give us wisdom to speak truth and to express ourselves with sincerity. Help us to be sensitive to others' hearts. You know that it is sometimes hard to forgive and be genuinely sorry for our actions. In fact, surely we make the same mistake with You! Help us try not to deceive ourselves or others. Most importantly, may we feel the joy of communing with You openly and honestly. Thank You that Your love for us is totally unconditional. In the name of Jesus we pray. Amen.

For Further Reflection

1. Think of a time that you said you were sorry but you were not. Did you feel comfortable with your apology?
2. Name some instances when you uttered hurtful words and never expressed regret. Are you sorry now? Why or why not?
3. Do you believe that Jesus went to the cross for *you*?
4. How do you demonstrate that you know you are forgiven?

19 | Swoosh!

May 11, 2020

Reagan and I have been very busy these days. Since the pandemic COVID-19 hit, we have spent lots of time on the computer doing school work. She is amazingly proficient with her computer keyboard skills. I am continually stunned with the amount of information and homework that is given to kindergarteners. This e-learning has really kept me on my toes. The terminology is very different for me. In math, I am learning about "decomposing" numbers. And I had forgotten that I could take pictures on the computer. We have to take pictures of all Reagan's work and upload it for the teacher to review. Reagan recently had to show me how to use the timer on the camera. I had no idea there was a timer. None.

For the most part, it has been fun learning together both inside and outside the house. We have taken nature walks for science and accomplished physical education assignments together. She is quite a little athlete. One day we decided to take our ball and go to a nearby basketball court. She carefully tried to maintain control of the ball and dribble it all the way there. That was impressive.

While we were both trying to make baskets, I began to make some suggestions. In my day, I was pretty good at the forward position in basketball and I was fairly consistent at being able to make baskets. To this day, my husband (Bampa) has yet to win a game of HORSE against me!

I instructed Reagan to keep her eye on the hoop and showed her how to use two hands and throw the ball underhand. She listened very carefully and did exactly as I told her and then SWOOSH! The ball did not even touch the rim. It was perfect! Both of us were stunned at her first-try success!

Pretty much with disbelief I asked, "Reagan, how did you do that?"

Without any hesitation at all, she replied, "I believed in myself."

Her reply took my breath away about as much as observing the perfect basket just seconds before. I loved that response and I silently wished that she could always maintain that same kind of positive attitude. How many people strive for that sort of outlook but never manage to achieve it?

If we approached every endeavor with that unwavering positivity, I am sure our success rates would be much higher. If we had the consistent mindset to believe that God believed in us, we would act with more confidence. We would not shy away from being bolder in our actions.

We can believe in ourselves because God believes in us. He created us so that we would prosper. The scripture in Jeremiah reminds us that harm was never part of God's plan. "'For I know the plans I have for you,' declares the LORD, 'plans to prosper you and not to harm you, plans to give you hope and a future'" (Jeremiah 29:11).

It is not a guarantee that we will always be able to swoosh the ball through the basket every time we say we believe in ourselves. However, knowing in whom we believe enables us to have confidence in all our undertakings because the Lord God Almighty is more than just a coach. He is our Savior and we have His Word to guard and guide us through every situation. That is a slam dunk for every circumstance. Swoosh!

Key Thought

God believes in us so we can believe in ourselves.

Scripture

"'For I know the plans I have for you' declares the LORD, 'plans to prosper you and not to harm you, plans to give you a hope and a future'" (Jeremiah 29:11).

Prayer

Dear Lord of all Creation, how mighty are Your wondrous works! Thank You for designing each one of us with our best interest in mind. Please help us to remember that You know us, believe in us, and love us. Our hearts are filled with gratitude for the care with which You knit us together. We desire to bring glory to You for Your perfect workmanship. With grateful hearts, we give You praise. Amen.

For Further Reflection

1. Do you trust that God believes in you?
2. Do you believe in yourself?
3. On a scale from one to ten, how would you rate your confidence level? Explain your answer.
4. When you were six years old, could you have declared, "I believed in myself!"?

20 | I Have Only 20 Minutes!

May 17, 2020

As a result of the prolonged coronavirus pandemic, I have continued to help Reagan with her school lessons. One of the most important aspects of e-learning with Reagan has been time management. We try very hard to maintain a good balance of doing schoolwork and taking breaks. Most often, she listens very well and we have no problems. We begin at about eight-thirty in the morning. The first subject we tackle is phonics because there are usually about four pages of work to complete and turn in. There are always videos of the teachers explaining what will be required. After each subject is completed, Reagan is entitled to a break.

Most often Reagan spends her time lying on my bed watching TV or playing a game on the computer. On this particular day, Reagan was engrossed with a favorite TV show. So, when Bampa came into the room to do his ritualistic teasing, Reagan became very upset with him. With an elevated voice she emphatically declared, "Ba-a-a-a-am-paaaa! Stop! I have only twenty minutes!"

She was right. I had informed her that she could take

a twenty-minute break. For the most part, we have been able to stick to our routine with that strategy. Reagan has understood the importance of having a schedule. She was very unhappy about Bampa's interruption.

We all know that it is important to be flexible but there are also many times that if we don't adhere to a schedule, we are not able to accomplish necessary tasks. Getting schoolwork finished is something that is non-negotiable.

For many, managing time is a big challenge because of so many other responsibilities. For some, having too much time frequently results in total mismanagement of it. At the end of the day, we ask ourselves where the time went and have absolutely nothing to show for it.

In this little scenario, I would be very curious to know what the responses would be if asked, "If you had only twenty minutes, how would you spend them?" I assume that many replies would be directly tied to what activity was taking place. If I were a runner, I would be taking a breather. If I were tied to a computer, I would choose to take a walk.

As we navigate through our daily routines, where does God fit in? Do we commune with Him throughout the day? Do we get up early or stay up later at night to converse with Him? Do we think that if we have already had our quiet time with Him, we are then able to check that off our list for the day?

In Reagan's case, her treat was to be able to watch TV. It was a reward for her hard work. I am wondering if we were working hard and were entitled to a twenty-minute break, would we consider spending time with the Lord our treat? For me, the times I have made that choice, I have been blessed. I feel His delight when we spend time together. And sometimes, that twenty-minutes can be more productive than anything else that occurred the entire day.

Key Thought

When time is precious, spending it with our Savior is always a good choice.

Scripture

"But when you pray, go into your room, close the door and pray to your Father, who is unseen. Then your Father, who sees what is done in secret, will reward you" (Matthew 6:6).

Prayer

Dear Heavenly Lord, You are the author of time. You have numbered our days and have ordained all that will happen in them. We thank you for the precious gift of time. Please help us to make wise choices with our time. And dear Lord, please help us to remember that spending time with You is the best way we could ever spend it! In Your holy name, we pray. Amen.

For Further Reflection

1. Have you ever regretted making the choice to spend time with Jesus, even when you had very limited time?
2. How much of a priority is it for you to spend time with Jesus?
3. How would you explain to another person what regular time with the Lord means to you?
4. Is it difficult or not for you to maintain a regular habit of Bible study? Prayer? Explain your response.

Gift of Time

Words and Lyrics by Deborah Denison Bailey

1. Through the years I realize more and more as time goes by. The clock ticks on, the more I see how time has been so good to me.
   (Bridge) For time has a way of healing things, and time has a way of forgiving and giving, - reliving.
2. Seasons change and so do I, to grow and learn, - more than survive. Winter time is when I reflect on all that's caused me some regret.
3. So complete the rose appears with those thorns that cause some tears. Beautiful the rose unfolds to share the wonder it beholds. It's joy in bloom now to perceive, this flower has grown in its own time and so fine, it's divine!

Chorus: Time shows me what I can be and then I see how precious is the gift of time! Time shows me what I can be. How precious is this precious gift of time!

Copyright July 20, 1992, #PAU 1-670-648.

21 | His Fingernail

June 19, 2020

While Reagan and I were sitting on my back porch visiting, she looked up at the sky and excitedly exclaimed, "Look Nana! The moon looks like God's fingernail!"

She was right. Somehow the moon was only partly visible and it did look like a fingernail. Naturally, because it was in the sky, it could only be God's fingernail we were seeing! Our conversation continued as she explained to me that it was "kind of like that song about the *whole world in His hands* except all we see is His fingernail."

I must admit that I was really pleased and touched that the first thing Reagan would think of was God when she looked up in the sky. That she would immediately remember the song about God holding the whole world told me that her belief system was already an integral part of her life.

When I look at Pikes Peak, I feel a resonance with the wonders of nature. It is not a huge stretch to have spiritual thoughts when I see such beauty. The challenge comes when things are not so lovely. For believers, often things that inspire us tend naturally to spawn religious thoughts.

The big question to entertain is how to keep God in all of

our routines – not just the ones that inspire us. He not only knows our every thought, He also sees and hears our every response, audible or not. How we react in all circumstances indicates the depth and sincerity of our faith.

We may display a vast array of inconsistencies. How we deal with the outcome of an event should prompt contemplation about how we are living. Do we try to live as Jesus would have us live? Do we sincerely try to see all things through His eyes? Do we listen for His voice to tell us when we are wrong? Do we truly believe we are forgiven when we ask for forgiveness?

All of these questions are ones to ponder thoughtfully. If we were really able fully to see the whole picture, there is a good chance we simply would not be able to handle it. Just seeing His thumbnail was quite enough of a glimpse to inspire some reflection. Praise be to God!

Key Thought

He's got the whole world in His hands.

Scripture

"In his hands are the depths of the earth, and the mountain peaks belong to him" (Psalm 95:4).

Prayer

Thank You, Lord, for having the whole universe in Your hands! We love and praise You for who You are and for Your presence which, while not always felt, sensed, or even acknowledged, is nonetheless present in the believer's life. As we live each day, may we be mindful of Your presence. Please guide our thoughts and our actions. May our responses bring glory to You in all circumstances we encounter. Help us seek to be more like You each day. In Christ's name we pray. Amen.

For Further Reflection

1. If God has the whole world in His hands, why do we have so many troubles?
2. What kinds of reactions do scenes in nature evoke? Awe? Fear? Worship? Other?
3. How do you maintain your perspective when situations in your personal life seem out of control?
4. When was the last time you thought you saw God's thumbnail, felt His nudge, or heard His whisper?

He's Got the Whole World in His Hands

Chorus: He's got the whole world in His hands. (x4)

1. He's got the itty-bitty baby in His hands. (x3)   He's got the whole world in His hands.
2. He's got a-you and me brother in His hands.(x3) He's got the whole world in His hands.
3. He's got a-you and me sister in His hands. (x3) He's got the whole world in His hands.

Source: LyricFind
Songwriters Geoffrey Love/Traditional
Sony/ATV Music Publishing LLC,
Warner Chappell Music, Inc

22 | COVID: The Refiner's Fire

August 9, 2020

The COVID 19 virus has pretty much brought a halt to most things. While Reagan and I were trying to figure out what we could go do together, we ended up making a list of things we wanted to do but couldn't because of the pandemic. On this particular day, we felt like going swimming but we did not have a reservation, so that activity was not possible. As she shrugged her shoulders and exhaled with a big sigh, she made a rather startling statement.

"Nana, I think God has the COVID virus here because He wants us to be stronger. He wants us to fight harder."

Wow! It never ceases to amaze me what comes out of the mouths of babes! What would prompt her to say that?

Our conversation did not stay very heavy for very long because other important things like my needing to know the names of the "My Little Ponies" living in "Equestria" were also very high on her list. However, she did make it abundantly clear that we all should try really hard to be strong. She insisted that if we could just "fight" harder, we would be successful. It was interesting to me that when she told me we needed to fight, she raised her arm and put up a firm fist.

As Reagan correctly stated, the desire to push and fight is usually a needed asset for success and is an admirable one when harnessed to an appropriate goal. I immediately think of all the hours of dedicated study and work that are required in all professions for achievement. There are also many people who "fight" just to survive the day. Persistence and endurance show up in all different shapes and sizes.

Rather than just being upset about the way the virus had disrupted her schedule, Reagan saw it as an opportunity to be stronger because of the challenge. Instead of being crippled by the circumstance, she was expressing ways to be made better by it. In spiritual terms, we might say it was a chance to be molded by the "Refiner's fire".

How many of us can say we enjoy the process of going through the proverbial fire? We may place different labels on it: pruning, shaping, molding. I am not sure I know anyone who actually relishes going through military basic training, but most would probably agree that the experience proved valuable.

I remember, when I was in the seventh grade, a U.S. Marine came to speak to our class. He explained what a difficult time he had had when he went through his initial training. He described being sleep deprived and unsure if he could endure it. In fact, he struggled and was held back from the on-time graduation. Apparently, those who were in charge must have appreciated his grit and determination and he did finish the course. He told us that the experience prepared him to be a better Marine. I remember looking at him as he stood straight and tall in front of our class and feeling great admiration for him.

We can summon the strength to face all sorts of obstacles when we put our trust in the One who creates, knows, and loves us. Jesus does not promise us an easy life. In fact, we are told that we will have tribulation. But because Jesus has overcome the world, our peace can be found in Him.

I am thankful that Reagan has the desire to push through and persevere when things are hard. I hope and pray that she will grow to understand that she does not have to rely upon her own strength. As she is being refined by the fire, she can learn to draw from the Lord's strength to withstand the heat.

Key Thought

The Lord's strength enables us to fight.

Scripture

"I have told you these things, so that in me you may have peace. In this world you will have trouble. But take heart! I have overcome the world" (John 16:33).

Prayer

Dear Heavenly Lord, we confess that we do not understand many of our trials. Our challenges are often very hard and sometimes we yield to the temptation to want to give up. But we know that You are Sovereign over all our circumstances. You are the only One who can protect us from ourselves and our situations. Our peace can only be found in You. We pray for Your protection and strength not only to endure our hardships but to thrive amidst them. Thank You for making what seems insurmountable entirely possible. In Your holy name we pray. Amen.

For Further Reflection

1. Was your response to the COVID virus anything like Reagan's?
2. Do you remember a "Refiner's fire" experience and the impact it had upon you?
3. What would have been your response to Reagan's comment?
4. Describe what it means to you to be at peace.

23 | Throw It Away? Really?

August 30, 2020

Most of us are familiar with sayings that tell us to beware what we say because it will come back to haunt us. Such was the case recently with my husband, affectionately referred to as Bampa, with words that were repeated back to him by Reagan.

Reagan and Bampa were having a great time playing in the pool together and things were going along "swimmingly" until Bampa decided he would squirt the water gun at Reagan. Of course, it was fine for her to go after him, but when he pursued her, it was another matter. When he blasted her with water, she was very irritated and blurted out in the most annoyed voice ever, "Bampa! Stop squirting me or I am going to take that water gun away from you and throw it away!"

Wow! I wonder where she had heard that!

Bampa enjoyed the biggest (silent) chuckle ever and agreed to stop squirting her. Then, interesting for me, he relayed the story with humorous detail and (strongly) suggested that I include the incident in my book. I was pleased that he thought it was important to add this story.

What lesson could be gleaned from that event? From my perspective, the account was yet another opportunity to write about the caution we must take with our words. Additionally, this occurrence illustrated to me the importance of following through with what we say we are going to do. I assume there are very few of us who have not been told that if we kept doing the wrong or annoying thing, a punishment would ensue. If that were said to us, was the warning ever carried out?

I have always believed that one of the strong messages in the Bible is that to the extent we are enlightened, we are accountable. Accordingly, when we are disobedient, we should expect discipline. We know also that even though God forgives us and loves us, He is a just and righteous God. That tells me that in order to be just, there are repercussions for unholy behavior. Countless examples of "tough love" are evident every single day. For example, "time-outs" are a very common way to address children's inappropriate behavior. However, confusion often results when parents convey to their children mixed messages which in turn often serve to exacerbate the problem.

When Reagan told Bampa that she would take the squirt gun and throw it away, she meant it! At least at the time she meant it. Once she realized that she would be throwing away her own toy, the threat most probably would not have stuck!

This story is meant to underscore the importance of saying what you mean and following through with the stated consequence. When we endeavor to align our behavior with God's Word, we can draw upon His strength to carry out His will in all circumstances. Does that mean that we sometimes need to follow through and throw away <u>our</u> toys?

Yes.

Key Thought

Say what you mean and follow through.

Scripture

"He who spares the rod hates his son, but he who loves him is careful to discipline him" (Proverbs 13:24).

Prayer

Thank You, dear Lord, for Your Word that gives us the instruction we need to lead a righteous life. Help us to choose our words carefully, especially with the young. May our words and actions be sources of light. Please help us to remember to seek Your guidance as we discipline those in our care. We desire to bring glory to You and Your holy name. Amen.

For Further Reflection

1. Think of a time when you said you were going to discipline a child and you didn't. Any regrets?
2. Is it difficult for you to apologize for things you should not have said?

3. Do you feel accountable to God for *all* your words and actions?
4. Put into your own words what it means to say that our Lord is just.

"No discipline seems pleasant at the time, but painful. Later on, however, it produces a harvest of righteousness and peace for those who have been trained by it."
Hebrews 12:11

24 | The Art

September 9, 2020

Today Reagan and I had the day off from doing on-line school learning so we decided that we would drive to some favorite places and enjoy our special break. We first went to the Garden of the Gods Park to take in the beautiful scenery on our exquisite weather day. We always love to go to the Balanced Rock area and climb around with all the other tourists. After taking lots of pictures, we then headed to Manitou Springs to purchase a cotton candy ice cream cone at a favorite creamery. We then walked to a nearby park, listened to music provided by the Colorado Springs Conservatory and enjoyed our yummy cones there.

Our next stop was to ride to Green Mountain Falls to see an outdoor art exhibit. It was provided by the *Green Box Project*. We were enthralled by the enormous balloon-like structures where some sort of looked like insects. They were odd, intriguing, and fun. Reagan seemed to be totally awed by the very different shapes.

The last thing we decided to do was go swimming. She always loves to do that. The pool was about fifty minutes away so we had plenty of time to chat in the car. In a very gentle yet admittedly prodding way, I asked her what had been her favorite activity. Without any hesitation at all, she said, "The art."

I have to confess that I did not expect that reply. After all, cotton candy ice cream and climbing on huge red rocks are both tremendous activities and totally appropriate for her age. The large art structures were nothing that she could relate to but she was obviously mesmerized by them, and inspired.

With a tone of seriousness, she very thoughtfully stated, "Nana, when I see art like that, it makes me feel like I want to paint like grown-ups do."

Actually, Reagan's teachers have already glowingly spoken about her artistic talents. She loves to draw, color and undertake all kinds of art projects. She mostly prefers to engage in art activities by herself. She does not want help. Instead, she takes great delight in surprising us all with her creations. She frequently tells us that she wants to be an artist. Truth be told, she already is!

Reagan probably did not know what the word "inspired" means though she surely knew what it felt like. She understood that something deep down inside prompted her to want to create art. She was resonating with the awesome way the Lord knit her together.

I think that faith does the same thing. Faith is something intangible. It is also what enables us to believe that all things are possible with God. Faith grows like the mustard seed and gives us the resources we need to go beyond ourselves - likewise, does art for many people. Inspiration and faith both are bigger concepts than most of us can fully grasp. Yet, we can relate to these umbrella words; and as we do, we catch a glimpse of God's overarching provision and greatness.

Key Thought

Pursue your passions.

Scripture

"For you created my inmost being; you knit me together in my mother's womb. I praise you because I am fearfully and wonderfully made; your works are wonderful, I know that full well" (Psalm 139:13-14).

Prayer

Thank You, Lord, for the unique way You created each one of us. Help us to honor the way You so carefully designed us. Although we can't see it, we know what inspiration looks and feels like. Likewise is faith also perceived and felt. Thank you for these tools that help us to know You better. With grateful hearts we pray in the precious name of Jesus. Amen.

For Further Reflection

1. What inspires you?

2. Why do you think the Lord created the arts and humanities? Be specific.
3. How do you personally define faith?
4. What or who helped you find and pursue your passions in life? Explain.

"Each one should use whatever gift he has received to serve others, faithfully administering God's grace in various forms."
1 Peter 4:10

25 | The Clean Earth Wins

October 10, 2020

I learned a big lesson today. I hope I will follow through on what I was taught by Reagan. I am so struck by her responsible attitude and the memories that her actions evoke in me, that I am trusting the experience will stick with me for a very long time.

Reagan recently had her seventh birthday and one of the things that she wanted was a basketball. I purchased a regulation-sized ball for her and afterwards I learned that basketballs come in smaller sizes for youngsters. We decided that we should go see how well she could handle a full-sized basketball. I instructed her to be very careful and to keep her eye on the basket. With a perfect underhanded throw, the ball swooshed through the hoop on the very first try. Wow! Perfect!

We were all set to have a very fun time together playing a game to see who could make the most baskets. But as we looked around the park area where we were playing, we noticed lots of carelessly discarded trash. Actually, it was mostly around the court where we were going to have our hoop competition. The thrill of the perfectly made basket became less important and our dismay about all the litter became the focal point.

Without any prompting, Reagan very seriously stated, "Nana it is more important to have the earth be clean than it is for us to stay here and play basketball. I think we should go back to your house, get gloves and a bag, and then come back and pick up this trash."

And so we did. We walked back to my house, got gloves and a bag, and walked back to the park and picked up trash. Most of the things we picked up were recyclable, like plastic water bottles. We filled the bag and made it back home in time for the garbage truck to take it all away. We both felt very pleased about our good deed.

As Reagan and I were picking up the litter, two very big, lingering thoughts came to me. First, I was reminded of the fact that I walk by this park literally all the time and yet I have never thought about doing anything about tidying up the litter routinely seen there. Actually, it is a lovely small neighborhood recreation area and it took relatively little effort or time to pick up the debris that was thoughtlessly strewn around. Why have I consistently ignored it?

My second thought centered around memories of my father. Dad regularly walked a couple of miles each day. As he walked, he collected trash and he very often found coins. My parents lived near a college campus and Dad would routinely walk through the parking lot of the campus and find lots of change there. He put the coins in a big jar and when it got full, he would put the money in the bank. He saved so much money that he was able to buy an airline ticket with it. He flew from North Carolina to Sedona, Arizona, to see the red rocks there. His conservation efforts literally paid off!

It would be wonderful if all people would be more responsible with their trash but that is just not the case. Those of us who care about honoring our surroundings and are in the position to do something about it, should. It is in the best interest of everyone when we do the right thing. I truly believe that the Lord smiles on those who protect and preserve His handiwork. The earth is His canvas and we have been entrusted to care for His creation. I have never understood how people could throw trash out the windows of their cars as they are driving down the highway. But they do.

I am so very thankful for the way God used Reagan to open my eyes to what I could so easily do to remedy the issue of litter in my neighborhood. The earth is the Lord's and everything in it! We honor Him when we preserve and protect His creation.

Had I had my wits about me during the clean-up, I would have recommended that she tidy her room!

Key Thought

We must all be good stewards of the Lord's creation.

Scripture

"The earth is the LORD'S and everything in it, the world, and all who live in it" (Psalm 24:1).

Prayer

Thank You, Lord, for the abundant blessings of Your creation! The entire earth with its vast resources is Your divine handiwork and we give You the glory for it. We desire to honor You as we protect and preserve Your creation. Please equip us with wisdom about how we can best be good stewards of Your provision. In the name of Jesus, we pray. Amen.

For Further Reflection

1. When you see litter strewn carelessly around, what is your response?
2. Do you recycle everything that you can? Why or why not?
3. Do you have any thoughts about how we could be more proactive in trying to encourage people not to litter?
4. I assume that there is a heavy emphasis in school about pollution and trash that has had a big impact upon Reagan. Do you think her response to clean up the litter she sees will grow or diminish with time? Explain.

For the Beauty of the Earth

Text: Folliott Sandford Pierpont
(1835-1917)
Music: Conrad Kocher,
(1786-1872)

Verse 1: For the beauty of the earth, For the beauty of the skies, For the love which from our birth, Over and around us lies, (Refrain)
Refrain: Lord of all to Thee we raise this our hymn of grateful praise.
Verse 2: For the beauty of each hour, Of the day and of the night, Hill and vale and tree and flow'r, Sun and moon and stars of light, (Refrain)
Verse 3: For the joy of human love, Brother, sister, parent, child, Friends on earth, and friends above, For all gentle thoughts and mild, (Refrain)
(Public Domain)

26 | The Thanksgiving Wreath

November 21, 2020

While Reagan and I have been doing the on-line school learning, we have had quite a few special projects to complete. One of those assignments was to make a Thanksgiving wreath. Mommy made it very easy for us because she gave us everything we needed for the project. All Reagan needed to do was to personalize the materials and put the wreath together. It was very easy for her to write down the things for which she was thankful. She loves her family and she loves her two dogs and her friends. Now how simple was that!

Reagan was having a sleepover at my house on that particular evening and that's always a very happy time. Before she goes to bed, we always snuggle and talk about the events of our day. As we were talking about the wreath we had made, Reagan said in a very thoughtful way, "You know Nana, everything we wrote to put on the wreath was true, but nothing is more important than God or Jesus. Nothing is more important than that."

I replied instantly, "You are right Reagan. Nothing is more important." We had not put God and Jesus on the wreath. We decided that was a serious omission.

We then made an easy decision to add the names of God and Jesus to our wreath. And what better place to put them than smack dab in the middle of the wreath! We thank God for our family and friends and everything else in this world and none of those things would be possible without our Lord and Savior.

Reagan was right to say that the names of God and Jesus needed to be on the wreath. It is here that I must admit that one of the reasons that I did not bring it up while we were making the wreath was because I had questions about how the school might react. That would have never entered my mind a few years ago; but sadly, it did that day.

I was wrong. I was dead wrong. I claim to embrace the entire gospel of Jesus Christ. And yet, I allowed myself to be a bit intimidated by a little voice saying that it might not be received very well to put Jesus and God on the wreath – in the center, no less!

When we took a picture of the wreath and turned it in on-line, the teacher quickly replied to Reagan to tell her that it was beautiful! I am assuming that the teacher was responding from her own heart. Whatever the case may be, Reagan was right to tell me that we had to fix the wreath. She already knows that Jesus and God make everything and we are thankful for them.

Key Thought

Never be ashamed to proclaim the name of the Lord!

Scripture

"I am not ashamed of the gospel, because it is the power of God for the salvation of everyone who believes: first for the Jew, then for the Gentile" (Romans 1:16).

Prayer

Forgive me, Lord, for entertaining the idea that I should back off from proclaiming what I know is true. You are Lord of all! Thank You for the words of wisdom spoken through a child. You make all things possible and we give You all the glory! In Your holy name we pray. Amen.

For Further Reflection

1. Has there been a time when you could have spoken about your faith but didn't because you were unsure about how your message would be received? Explain.
2. If you have been bold about your faith in a challenging circumstance and the response was disappointing, how did it affect your thoughts about future encounters?
3. Do you think there are circumstances when it is absolutely not appropriate to discuss your faith? If so, what are they?
4. Have you ever led a person to accepting Jesus as personal Savior? What was the experience like for you?

Reagan's Thanksgiving Wreath
Made by Reagan Bailey
Photo by Deborah Denison Bailey, 2020

27 | "My Heart"

November 24, 2020

Reagan and I always have a great experience when we go to the pool and swim. After we have had a wonderful time and are changing back into our clothes, we often have a race to see who will be dressed first. As she is finishing dressing, I frequently end up helping her to get the tangles out of her hair.

On this particular day, we started talking about our bodies. When she asked me if I knew what parts of her body she liked the best, I was stunned by her answer.

"Nana, I like my hair and my heart the best."

Naturally, I asked her why she had made those particular choices. I could understand the answer about her hair but I was curious about her heart answer. What would make her say that?

Reagan very simply and eloquently stated, "Nana, I like my hair because I would not like to be bald. I like my heart because that is what God sees. He knows me because of my heart."

Wow! Together we have talked a lot about Jesus living in her heart. We have also sung a song many times entitled

"Down in My Heart" which is all about the joy of Jesus living in her heart. Obviously, she has remembered that song and our conversations. What a joy it was for me to hear her once again remind me that Jesus was in her heart and that He was listening. She already knows that Jesus knows and loves her. That is absolutely thrilling!

Reagan will learn more about the peace and love that can reside deep within her as she matures. But for my money, she is already way ahead of many. I am trusting that the relationship that she has begun with Jesus living in her heart will continue to grow and flourish.

Key Thought

Jesus lives in our hearts.

Scripture

"But the LORD said to Samuel, 'Do not consider his appearance or his height, for I have rejected him. The LORD does not look at the things man looks at. Man looks at the outward appearance, but the LORD looks at the heart'" (1 Samuel 16:7).

Prayer

Thank You, Lord Jesus, for the precious thoughts that Reagan shared today. Out of the mouth of this babe was a simple truth that we all can know and trust. The love of Jesus is our greatest gift. It will endure and last forever.

May we always remember that from the moment we accept Jesus as our Savior, we are forever companions. Thank You for living in our hearts. Lord Jesus, we praise You for all that You are forever and always. Amen.

For Further Reflection

1. When was the first time you heard that Jesus lives in your heart and how did you respond?
2. Do you think it is a difficult concept to understand when you learn that Jesus looks at your heart to know you?
3. How would you explain to a child what joy in your heart feels like?
4. What kinds of adjectives do you use to explain Jesus living in your heart?

28 | My Little Valentine

January 13, 2021

All the holiday festivities have come to an end and school is back in session. Actually, learning is happening again but it's still on-line because of COVID. Reagan and I are trying very hard to get back into a routine that is conducive to studying.

Now that Christmas is over, Reagan is already looking forward to the next holiday. She was hoping that her birthday would be the next big event. But then she remembered that her birthday was in the Fall and that was a long way off. As she was trying to remember the celebrations that take place each month, she became very excited to recall that Valentine's Day was in February.

As soon as she realized that Valentine's Day was coming up, her first response was, " Nana, that means that I need to make something for four people." She raised her arm up and displayed four fingers and pointed to each finger with her pointer finger on the other hand as she said, "Nana, Bampa, Mommy, and Daddy."

I more than received my valentine gift when she expressed her desire to do something for those she loved.

As I think about it, I am a little surprised and very delighted that the first thing that came to Reagan's mind was to do something nice for the people she listed. I'm guessing that most little kids would first think about candy – especially chocolate!

As I am writing this, I am just now remembering that just before Christmas Reagan was adamant that I take her shopping for presents for her neighborhood friends. While we were in the store selecting gifts, she was very careful to select items that would appeal to older kids. All of them are at least three years older than Reagan and she knew that "little kid" toys would not be appropriate for them.

Reagan has a giving heart. She is truly delighted when she can make someone happy. She frequently displays that in a myriad of ways. My Little Valentine is His, too.

Key Thought

The Lord knows our hearts.

Scripture

"As water reflects a face, so a man's heart reflects the man" (Proverbs 27:19).

Prayer

Dear Lord, You know us because You created us. You listen to our hearts and determine if we are the honoring people You created us to be. Please help us strive to be all that You intended for us to become. We wish to bring glory to you through our words and our actions. We trust You for that guidance. In Your holy name we pray. Amen

For Further Reflection

1. How does it make you feel to know that the Lord knows you because He sees your heart?
2. Do you ever entertain the idea that you can hide your thoughts from God?
3. What are you hoping that the Lord sees in your heart?
4. Do you think it is really possible to "love one another"?

"Even a child is known by his actions, by whether his conduct is pure and right."
Proverbs 20:11

"The heart is deceitful above all things and beyond cure. Who can understand it?"
Jeremiah 17:10

29 | $10 \times 3 + 7 = 37$

January 24, 2021

Reagan loves marshmallows. When she drinks hot chocolate, she always asks if I have marshmallows. On this particular day, she brought the bag of small marshmallows to me and asked how many she could have. I looked at her and said, "Since you are seven years old, you may have seven."

That was fine with her and she turned around and began to leave. But as she started to walk away, she turned back around and looked at me straight in the eye and very directly stated, "Nana, I ate ten marshmallows three times and now I have seven. That makes thirty-seven marshmallows."

Obviously Reagan felt the strong need to come clean on the total number of marshmallows she had gotten. In fact, she very consistently demonstrates to me that telling the whole truth is very important to her. She knew that there was something not quite right about not telling me about the thirty marshmallows she had already consumed. Since she is currently learning about adding tens in math, I think she was also rather pleased about announcing the sum! I thanked her for telling me the truth and she then merrily walked away with her hot chocolate brimming with the seven marshmallows.

This simple story is meant to drive home an important lesson. Telling the truth is as important when dealing with small things as it is with big things. I would never have known about the thirty marshmallows Reagan had already eaten if she had not told me. She would have known though, and consequently, it mattered to her. I wonder if other seven- year-old children would have been quite so honest about the marshmallows. Would they have been afraid to tell the truth? Reagan was forthright in her confession and showed no signs of trepidation.

I think Reagan is so straightforward with me because we have an established relationship based upon trust. We also are incredibly sensitive to each other's hearts. The bond that we share is extraordinarily strong because we both intentionally and consistently demonstrate to each other that our love for one another is what matters most. We can handle all the tosses and turns that come our way because we are committed to being honest with each other. That's why, with eyes wide open to receive whatever response I chose to make, Reagan could be honest with me about the actual number of marshmallows. If I had really been on my toes, I probably would have said to her, "Why don't you have ten more!" Then, we could have continued on to learn in our math lesson that ten, four times, equals forty!

Key Thought

Honesty is the best policy.

Scripture

"A truthful witness gives honest testimony" (Proverbs 12:17).

Prayer

Heavenly Lord, we are so thankful for all the lessons You provide for us to receive. Who would have thought that so much spiritual nutrition could be gained from a cup of hot chocolate! Your provision is so abundant and so amazing! Thank You for creating in us hearts that are capable of being open to give and to receive. Please help us to grow in relationship with You so that we will be equipped to receive all the lessons You have planned for us. With grateful hearts, we pray in the name of Jesus. Amen.

For Further Reflection

1. Have you ever feared that telling the truth would hurt your relationship with someone? Explain.
2. How do you summon courage to face difficult tasks?
3. Personalize the scripture, "A truthful witness gives honest testimony."
4. Would you have given Reagan more marshmallows?

30 | You are Special

February 13, 2021

I am very intentional about telling Reagan about how much I love her. It is my total joy to convey to her how much I truly adore her. She always tells me that she knows that I love her a lot.

Included in all the conversation about the many ways I love her, there are statements like, "Reagan, you are smart. Reagan, you are fun. Reagan, you are kind. Reagan, you are artistic. Reagan, you have a great imagination. Reagan, I think you are the sweetest girl in the whole world!" I very purposefully say her name when I make these statements.

Recently, after I had gone through this ritual, she looked at me with very probing eyes and asked, "Nana, do you think I am special?"

I replied with astonishment, "Reagan, I tell you all the time how much I love you and I tell you all the things that are so wonderful about you."

Reagan then very thoughtfully replied, "Yes, Nana, I know you tell me those things but you don't say that I am special."

It was obviously very important to hear the word, "special". All the attributes I listed to describe her were not enough. They were not conveying to her that she was special. She obviously needed to hear it and I am very puzzled and bothered about this.

Since no human being is exactly the same, I know that we are all unique. Unique sounds like a more "special" word than different. And to me, the word "special" sounds more "special" than unique. Perhaps it's my personal feelings that make me know that she is special. Because she is special to me, does that make her special?

In scripture, we are told that we were all uniquely designed by God. In fact, nothing created by God was exactly duplicated the same way. It is amazing to me that even snowflakes are all different. However, I am not sure that it can be said that just because snowflakes are different, they are necessarily special.

Do all the qualities I listed about Reagan make her special? I think that is exactly what she wanted to know. Is she special because of all of the things that are considered positive? That would imply that when she is not the fun, loving, good little girl, she is no longer special.

Scripture reveals to us that we are all created in God's image. We also know we have been "...fearfully and wonderfully made" (Psalm 139:14). That is wondrously amazing and what truly makes all of us special!

As I think about it, I am also realizing that what makes us special is the way we honor God in the unique ways He created us. We glorify Him when we use our talents and abilities the way He would have us do. When we love others as well as ourselves, we demonstrate His love for us. We are all special in God's eyes. After all, we are His beautiful creation and everything that God does is good. It is up to us first to acknowledge this truth and then share it with "special" reminders to ourselves and others. From this day forward I plan repeatedly to remind Reagan that she is special, and why.

Key Thought

You are special!

Scripture

"I praise you because I am fearfully and wonderfully made; your works are wonderful, I know that full well" (Psalm 139:14).

Prayer

Thank you, dear Heavenly Lord, for the wonders of all creation. We are blessed to have been created by You. You have endowed us with unique abilities and we wish to use those talents to serve You. Please help us know how best to do that. Help us in our daily walk to remember that we are loved and we are special. In the powerful name of Jesus we pray. Amen.

For Further Reflection

1. Do you feel special?
2. Is it easy or difficult for you to embrace the concept of being special?
3. Is it easier to think of other people as special, rather than yourself? Explain.
4. If you were asked to describe to Reagan why she is special, what would you say?
5. Look for a "specialty" in every person!

31 | Breathe. Focus. Strike!

February 28, 2021

My husband, Paul (aka Bampa), and I are on a bowling team. Sometimes our scores are very good and other times, they are alarmingly awful. To simply say that we are very inconsistent is an understatement. In fact, the name of our bowling team is *The Unpredictables.* I just looked up synonyms for our name and they were "random", "changeable", and "erratic". We could not have a more appropriate team name!

School was cancelled because of weather so Reagan was with us as we were playing our three games of bowling. She dutifully sat at the table and did some homework while Bampa and I were bowling. By the time the third game rolled around, Reagan was finished with her studies and became increasingly interested in how we were doing. When Bampa throws the ball, it goes down the alley very fast and all the pins literally splatter. My execution is not at all as exciting. I had managed to hold my own in the first two games but the third round was less than disappointing. It was a disaster.

After I had thrown another terrible ball, I went back

to the table where Reagan was sitting and muttered something that reflected that I was doing an awful job and I was very frustrated. As Reagan looked at me, I could see that she was very conscientiously mulling over what she could say to encourage me. With all the authority that a seven-year-old could possibly muster, she became my coach and declared, "Nana, you have to breathe and Nana, you have to focus." She looked directly into my eyes and never moved hers. While she was instructing me on what I needed to do, she lifted both of her hands parallel to either side of her face as she illustrated to me that nothing should be allowed to distract me. In other words, she was demonstrating the equivalent of blinders that are put on horses when they race.

Maybe it was luck, or maybe it was her expert instruction, but I got a strike in the very next frame! We were both very pleased! When I went back to celebrate with her the success I had just had, Reagan then was very interested in knowing if she had helped me. She asked, "Nana, did my telling you what to do help you a lot or a little?"

It was important for Reagan to know not only that her coaching was useful, but also that it felt supportive for me. Again, she never moved her eyes until she received my answer. Naturally, I told her that she was extremely helpful. I must admit that as I was advancing to throw the bowling ball, I was thinking about Reagan. I knew she was watching. I also was very aware that she really calmed me down and had given me sage advice. When I affirmed to her that her coaching was beneficial, it made her very happy.

Our Lord is delighted when we respond to Him. He longs to hear our hearts. Whether we think He has helped us a little, a lot, or not at all, He longs for our communication with Him because He loves us so much. It is always all about the relationship. When we make it a priority to focus on Him, our relationship can't help but grow deeper. He waits because He loves us.

We all know it is not always easy. How do we quiet ourselves so that we are able to focus? How do we pray when we feel scattered and so frustrated that finding words to express our dilemma feels impossible? One way is just to start breathing purposefully. The One who gave us breath promises to be faithful to us. The Lord has never taken His eyes off us. He knows us, loves us, and promises to guide us through all circumstances in our lives. It is true that He even cares enough to speak through a child during a bowling game. When we keep our focus on Him, He is faithful to guide our every step.

The advice that Reagan gave me applies to every circumstance in life. The advice to breathe is something that our bodies perform without our having to think about it. Yet, when we do, it calms us, centers us, and enables us to become more attentive. As we endeavor fully to engage in the focusing function, we are better equipped to block out distractions. The odds of succeeding are greatly increased when we follow those steps. When we choose to focus upon seeking the Lord's will for our lives, we are always honoring Him. When bowling, it could very well result in a strike!

Key Thought

Breathe. Focus.

Scripture

"As long as I live, while I have breath from God, my lips will speak no evil, and my tongue will speak no lies" (Job 27:3-4).

Prayer

Thank You, Lord, that you never let us out of Your sight! From the moment the breath of life was breathed into us, You have been with us. Sometimes we feel Your presence and sometimes we don't. But we always trust that You are with us. Help us, dear Lord, to share our hearts fully with You. We know that is what You desire of us. We praise You for Your goodness and Your faithfulness! In the blessed name of Jesus we pray. Amen.

For Further Reflection

1. How difficult is it for you to concentrate on your breathing?
2. What techniques do you employ to help you to focus?
3. How do you maintain your focus when you are listening for God?
4. Do you believe that the Lord never loses His focus on you? Explain.

A STRIKE!!
Drawing by Reagan M. Bailey, 2021

This second book is part of a continuing series by Deborah (Debbie) Denison Bailey. In addition to her writing, she is an accomplished vocalist and has enjoyed many endeavors during her career as a Music Director, Music Therapist, Activity Director, Nursing Home Administrator and Adjunct College Instructor.

Deborah has been married to Paul (Bampa) for forty-seven years. They are proud parents of a son, daughter and granddaughter, Reagan. Deborah and Paul have enjoyed travel to many places in most of the US, Europe and several locations in Asia and Africa.

Colorado Springs has been their home base for the majority of their marriage, except for retreats from the cold when they head south. Deborah's hobbies include walking, swimming, attending concerts, gardening, beaching, and composing. As enjoyable to Deborah as her hobbies is her commitment to extending a kindness to someone each day.

Individual and group Bible study remains a top priority for Deborah. It is also important to her to maintain close contact with dear friends and family. Quality living necessitates quality relationships.

Acknowledgements

My gratitude for Velma Kreiger is enormous! Her continuous support for my "Divine Directions" series has been monumental. She has provided both editing expertise and helpful insight. I thank her for generously sharing my efforts with many people through her book ministry. Her love of the Lord has been unselfishly demonstrated through the many ways she has encouraged and promoted my work.

I offer my sincere appreciation to Megan Denison Smith, for her generous offering of the drawing, *Devil Sitting on a Thumbtack.*

End Notes

All scriptural references were obtained from the *Women of Faith Study Bible,* New International Version, Copyright 2001 by the Zondervan Corporation, Library of Congress # 00-133720

Benjamin Franklin quote: BrainyQuote.com

Corrie ten Boom quote: Quotepark.com, Source: Clippings from My Notebook, Public Domain

Megan Denison Smith – Release of Rights for "Devil Sitting on a Thumbtack"

Printed in the United States
by Baker & Taylor Publisher Services